# Pearson Scott Foresman
# Writing Rubrics and Anchor Papers

Glenview, Illinois
Boston, Massachusetts
Chandler, Arizona
Upper Saddle River, New Jersey

ISBN-13: 978-0-328-47655-8
ISBN-10: 0-328-47655-2

6 7 8 9 10 V031 15 14 13 12 11

# Contents

## Writing Models

## Weekly Rubrics

# Support for Writing

## Suggestions for Using This Book

This book is most effective when used in conjunction with the weekly writing lessons and unit writing process lessons in Scott Foresman's *Reading Street*. Rubrics and anchor papers can be copied and distributed or made into transparencies. Here are some ways to use the materials.

- Distribute copies of page v to students. Work through the explanations of traits with the class to develop background for discussing scores.

- Display one-by-one the four models for a given mode in order (starting with Score 1 or Score 4). Work through the commentaries that appear along with the models to illustrate how each got its score.

- After students become proficient with determining scores, distribute copies of writing models from this book with the scores screened out. Work with students to arrive at scores.

- Display a model that is Score 1. Work with students to improve the model.

- Display the rubric for the type of writing you are teaching. Have students use the rubric to evaluate their own writing.

- Distribute copies of the Self-Evaluation Guide on page vi. Have students use this guide to evaluate their work.

## Tips for Teaching and Evaluating Writing

- Choose one writing trait to emphasize each week. Appoint a team of students for each trait. Have them find their trait in selections they read and in their own writing and present their findings to the class.

- Read short passages from literature (for example, a tall tale) and from other content areas (for example, a science text). Point out how writer's purpose determines voice, word choice, and style.

- Remember that a writer may be more proficient in one trait than in another. To arrive at a score, evaluators must weigh proficiency in all traits.

- Tell students that when they evaluate their own writing, assigning a score of 3, 2, or even 1 does not necessarily indicate a failure. The ability to identify areas for improvement in future writing is a valuable skill.

- Encourage students to think of themselves as writers. Alert them that subjects, words, and ideas are everywhere. Suggest they keep a notebook handy to record material, such as overheard conversations, sentences from their reading, and vivid words they encounter.

- Join students as they write. Share your own writing with them and ask for their feedback on your work.

- Model constructive ways of giving feedback on writing. *(Words such as* pounce *and* swat *give me a good picture of your cat. You said her name is Boots. How did she get that name? You mentioned that she has a favorite place to sleep. Could you describe it?)*

# Writing Traits

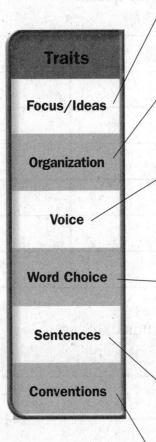

**Traits**

- Focus/Ideas
- Organization
- Voice
- Word Choice
- Sentences
- Conventions

- **Focus/Ideas** refers to the main purpose for writing and the details that make the subject clear and interesting. It includes development of ideas through support and elaboration.

- **Organization** refers to the overall structure that guides readers through a piece of writing. Within that structure, transitions show how ideas, sentences, and paragraphs are connected.

- **Voice** shows the writer's unique personality and establishes a connection between writer and reader. Voice, which contributes to style, should be suited to the audience and the purpose for writing.

- **Word Choice** is the use of precise, vivid words to communicate effectively and naturally. It helps create style through the use of specific nouns, lively verbs and adjectives, and accurate, well-placed modifiers.

- **Sentences** covers strong, well-built sentences that vary in length and type. Skillfully written sentences have pleasing rhythms and flow fluently.

- **Conventions** refers to mechanical correctness and includes grammar, usage, spelling, punctuation, capitalization, and paragraphing.

# Self-Evaluation Guide

Name _____

Name of Writing Product _____

**Directions** Review your final draft. Then rate yourself on a scale from 4 to 1 (4 is a top score) on each writing trait. After you fill out the chart, answer the questions.

| Writing Traits | 4 | 3 | 2 | 1 |
|---|---|---|---|---|
| Focus/Ideas | | | | |
| Organization | | | | |
| Voice | | | | |
| Word Choice | | | | |
| Sentences | | | | |
| Conventions | | | | |

1. What is the best part of this piece of writing? Why do you think so?

   _____

   _____

   _____

2. Write one thing you would change about this piece of writing if you had the chance to write it again.

   _____

   _____

   _____

# Writing Models

**PROMPT** ▶ **Write about a time you were in a new place or situation. Tell what happened and how you felt as a newcomer.**

| Rubric | 4 | 3 | 2 | 1 |
|---|---|---|---|---|
| **Focus/Ideas** | Personal narrative well focused and developed with many supporting details | Personal narrative generally focused and developed with supporting details | Personal narrative often off topic; lacks enough supporting details | Personal narrative without focus or sufficient information |
| **Organization** | Clear sequence of events with time-order words | Reasonably clear sequence with one or two lapses | Confused sequence of events | Incoherent sequence or no sequence of events |
| **Voice** | Natural-sounding conversational voice that expresses feelings | Pleasant voice that somewhat expresses feelings | Weak voice with little language expressing feelings | Dull writing with no clear voice or expression of feeling |
| **Word Choice** | Vivid descriptive words that show instead of tell | Some vivid words that show instead of tell | Few vivid words that show instead of tell | No attempt to show instead of tell |
| **Sentences** | Clear sentences, varied in type and style | Mostly clear sentences with some variety | Some sentences unclear; little variety | Incoherent sentences; dull, choppy style |
| **Conventions** | Few, if any, errors | Several minor errors | Errors that detract from writing | Serious errors that prevent understanding |

## How to Make Friends

This was terrible! I looked out the window on my first morning in Springfield. It was a Saturday, but no one was in sight. Just rows and rows of houses full of strangers. I had to start school on Monday, I didn't know anyone, and my stomach was fluttering. What was I going to do?

Mom said, "I'm tired of hearing you whine, Max." She told me to take the dog for a walk and give her some peace to unpack. I snapped the leash on Toby's collar and started along the street, trying to look like I knew where I was going.

I should tell you that Toby is a big strong Labrador, and he was pretty excited to be in a new neighborhood. He pranced along the sidewalk like a puppy. Suddenly he saw a cat. Zoom! Toby launched himself like a rocket across someone's lawn. I took off after him at the other end of the leash. The cat squeezed through a fence. Toby followed, but his head got stuck. Still holding the leash, I tried to yank him back.

That's how I met Pete. He was on the other side of the fence, playing catch with his dad. When Pete and his dad saw Toby's head wedged in their fence, they started to

Continued on next page

laugh. And after a while, so did I.

It turned out that Pete wanted a dog more than anything. What's more, he went to my school. Suddenly, the world wasn't so scary anymore. When I got home, my mom said I should take the dog out more often!

## Score 4

Readers are immediately drawn into this narrative with a clear beginning, middle, and end. The writer expresses his feelings. *(Suddenly, the world wasn't so scary anymore.)* He speaks directly to readers in a friendly voice. *(I should tell you…)* Vivid descriptive words *(fluttering, snapped, pranced, launched, squeezed, yank, wedged)* enliven the narrative. Sentences are of different lengths and types (declarative, interrogative, and exclamatory). There are simple, compound, and complex sentences. Fragments are used where appropriate, along with an interjection *(Zoom!)*

# Skiing

When my parents told me that we were going downhill skiing I was excited. We were headed for a hockey tournament in New Richmond. My first game was on Saturday, but we left on Thursday night, so we had an extra day to ski on Friday in Wausau, Wisconsin. I thought the ski hill would be a lot bigger than it was. When we got there I was surprised. Out instructor was named Jean. I stayed close to her. I couldn't miss her bright pink parka and yellow earmuffs.

We started on bunny hills. My brother looked funny hitting the orange practice cones down. I did a good job at swirrving down the hill. I "crashed" a few times. It snowed a lot the night before, so there was about five inches of "powder" as they call it. It was scary going up the hill in the chairlift because I had about two seconds to jump into the seat, and it is about 100 feet in the air. Getting off was easy because my dad helped me. Going down the bigger hill for the first time was exciting. I didn't use any poles. I zoomed down the hill. It got much easier after the first few times. Granite Peak ski hill was a new and enjoyable experience.

Continued on next page

## Score 3

The writer communicates the excitement of skiing for the first time. Word choice is sometimes specific and vivid *(bright pink parka, yellow earmuffs, zoomed)*. Some short, choppy sentences beginning with *I* could be combined for a smoother style. The two complex sentences in paragraph one should have a comma after the introductory clause. There is a misspelled word *(swirrving)*.

## Summer School

I'm going to tell you about summer school.

When we arrived at school, my mother gave my little brother Kyle, and my cousin Vivian and I our breakfast and walked Kyle to his class. Vivian and I walked to the auditorium. Vivian went to the entering 2nd grade group in the auditorium, and I went to my group in the auditorium. We sang songs.

Next I went to a classroom. There the other kids and I had a snack. Then the teacher read us a story. After that we did an activity based on the story.

It was soon dismissal time. My class walked downstairs and through a door leading to the outside. When we sat down out there, Vivian and I talked until my mom came.

I got in the car with Vivian and Kyle. Mom asked me how my day was. I said, "Good!" I couldn't wait 'til tomorrow as we drove off to get lunch.

Continued on next page

## Score 2

The narrative has a clear beginning, middle, and end. However, it is unclear whether this situation was a new one for the writer, and she gives little information to explain how she feels about her experience. The writer seems to have good control of basic sentence structure, but voice is flat, and many sentences have similar structures.

One day when I went over to my friend Julia's birthday party, I was the last one there and I didn't know any one but her family. Then when everyone else was having fun, I just sat in the corner and watched. We went to the movie. After we got back they got ready for bed (it was a sleepover) and I called my mom. I felt bad when I saw her face. I got all sad because I always do that. The next day I asked her if she minded me going home, she said no.

Continued on next page

## Score 1

This narrative lacks development and specific details. The overuse of pronouns causes confusion about who the writer is referring to. Conventions errors include a lack of punctuation and paragraph indention.

**PROMPT** Write about how a real team of people worked together to achieve a goal.

| Rubric | 4 | 3 | 2 | 1 |
|---|---|---|---|---|
| **Focus/Ideas** | Expository composition well focused and well supported by facts | Expository composition generally focused and supported with some facts | Expository composition poorly focused; few facts | Expository composition without focus; no facts |
| **Organization** | Well organized; clear introduction, body, and conclusion | Organized, with an introduction, body, and conclusion | Lacking clear introduction, body, and conclusion | Not organized |
| **Voice** | Conversational tone; knowledgeable writer | Engaging voice but lacks expertise | Uncertain voice | Dull writing with no clear voice |
| **Word Choice** | Uses precise words for clear meaning | Uses some precise words | Uses few precise words | No attempt to use precise words |
| **Sentences** | Clear sentences; no run-ons | Mostly clear sentences | Some sentences unclear | Incoherent sentences or short choppy sentences |
| **Conventions** | Few, if any, errors | Several minor errors | Frequent errors | Errors that hamper understanding |

## Stopping the River

Last year, there was a flood along the Hallam River that runs right by our town. There are many buildings and homes near the banks of the river, and the people in town worked together to keep the river from flooding.

Storms

The floods were caused by thunderstorms. It rained almost every day for three weeks in a row and the river kept rising higher and higher. People started to get nervous. If the rain didn't stop soon, they knew the river would flood and many houses and buildings would be ruined.

Making a Decision

Finally, Mayor Severin and some other people decided that they should start sand bagging the river. Sand bagging is filling up many hundreds, even thousands, of bags with sand and stacking them by the river. When you do this, it can help keep a town or house from flooding. It's almost like putting up a wall that will help hold the water.

Working Together

Almost everyone in town came to help with sand bagging. Some people were sand bagging to keep their own houses from being flooded. But most people were there because

Continued on next page

they wanted to help the town. There were kids my age and even younger helping. Some people came from farms or other towns nearby to help us too. There was something for everyone to do. Some people couldn't help with sand bagging, so they made food for people, or helped in other ways. It was hard work, but it was also fun too sometimes.

Goal Achieved

Two days later the water level started to go back down. The river never did flood, but it came close. If it had, our town would have been ready for it! We worked together to achieve our goal!

## Score 4

This composition is focused and organized with an introduction, body, and conclusion. The tone is conversational and knowledgeable, and word choice is precise and appropriate to the writing task. Sentences are mostly varied and well constructed. There is good control of conventions.

## My Gymnastics Team

My gymnastics team had to work together to acheive a goal. Our goal was to perform our very best at our state meet. We had to work hard by practicing and encourageing each other.

Each member of the team showed up to practice three days a week. Everyone spent three hours at each practice working on the routines for all the events we were competing in. We had people competing in four events: beam, bars, floor, and vault. If something went wrong, we didn't give up. Each team member would put in extra practice every day to try to make sure that we didn't make mistakes.

Another way we worked together was by encourageing each other. In practice, if one member was having trouble getting their routine down, there was always another person there to tell her what she was doing rite and give her encouragement. Whenever any of the team members was about to compete at their event the other team members would always say things like "Your going to be great!" We all did our best to work together as a team and we cheered

Continued on next page

each other on. This is important when you are a member of a team.

　　We competed, and our gymnastics team earned second place all around at the state meet.　Even though we didn't win first place we were still very proud of each other. We all performed at our very best, so we acheived our goal!

## Score 3

This composition fulfills the prompt. It is well focused, organized, and supported with facts. It has a clear introduction, body, and conclusion. The tone is conversational and enthusiastic and the writer is knowledgeable. However, misspellings *(acheive, encourageing, rite, your* for *you're)* and comma omissions in compound and complex sentences keep this composition from earning the highest score.

## A New House

An eight-year-old girl named Jenessa has given many smiles to kids that are battling cancer by giving them a single toy, but she is going through the same disease. To make matters worse, Jenessa has a moldy, torn up home.

A home makeover team is a team that builds extraordinary homes for hard working people that really deserve it like Jenessa and her family. The team sent the family on vacation while they made over their house.

Outside and inside the team made the house was modern and uniqe. Janessa's bedroom was like a mall. She had manequins just like she had requested. Her walls were pink and black. Jenessa's closet was filled with dress up clothes and designer shoes.

Jenessa's 13-year-old brother's room had wooden boxes with every video game systems you could imagine. Jenessa's 14-year-old brother room had his art work displayed everywhere, and comics were all over his room!

Jenessa's parents' room was astonishing. Everything was wood!! The floors, the walls, and the ceiling were all wood! It took an enormus amount of time, but in the back yard

Continued on next page

the makeover team built a pond with fish in it and a bridge over it.

When the family saw there house they teared up, especially Jenessa. This amazing makeover team made a great house for the family in only 7 days.

## Score 2

This composition does include an introduction, body, and conclusion, but it does not appropriately address the prompt. The writer does not explain how the team worked together to achieve a goal; rather the explanation is about the end result. Conventions errors include misspellings *(uniqe, manequins, enormus, there* for *their)*, a missing comma after an introductory phrase, an agreement mistake *(with every video game systems you could imagine)* and a missing possessive *(Jenessa's 14-year-old brother room).*

### Fire Fitters

"Yes sir, we have a house fire." "OK I can help." "Suit up Boys" Once they get ever thing ready they can head out to save lives. Then the sirens started to ring and all the cars moved out of the way, so that they could get to the fire quickly. They speed to the burning flames. They get all the hoses out so they can spray the flames down. Then take many safety pro cotions. They spray it down. Once the fire is almost out they hear a whine. So they have to send a man in to save him. first they have to get the mans gas mask so he can breeth. Then he goes in he keeps low so he can breath. Then he has to find the little boy. Once he finds him he has to save him. He picks him up and carries him out.

Continued on next page

## Score 1

This composition focuses on firefighters, but there is no introduction or conclusion; it is written like a story. A lack of pronoun referents causes some confusion about what is happening. There is a run-on sentence *(Then he goes in he keeps low so he can breath.)*, misspelled words *(Fitters, ever thing* instead of *everything, pro cotions, breeth* and *breath* instead of *breathe)*, lack of appropriate formatting for dialogue, missing commas after two introductory phrases as well as two compound sentences, and a sentence that does not begin with a capital letter.

**PROMPT** Write about how two animals are alike and different.

| Rubric | 4 | 3 | 2 | 1 |
|---|---|---|---|---|
| **Focus/Ideas** | Compare and contrast essay clearly focused | Compare and contrast essay generally focused | Compare and contrast essay lacking focus | Compare and contrast essay without focus |
| **Organization** | Clear structure of similarities and differences with transition words | Reasonably clear structure of similarities and differences; few transition words | Faulty structure; few transition words | No identifiable structure of similarities and differences; no transition words |
| **Voice** | Informative, engaging voice | Engaging but lacks expertise | Voice uncertain | Dull writing with no clear voice |
| **Word Choice** | Uses strong verbs to elaborate details | Uses some strong verbs to elaborate details | Uses few strong verbs | Uses no strong verbs |
| **Sentences** | Variety of well-structured sentences | Some well-structured sentences | Few well-constructed sentences | Contains fragments and run-ons |
| **Conventions** | Few or no errors | Some errors | Many errors that detract from writing | Serious errors that hamper understanding |

## The American Alligator and the Komodo Dragon

The American alligator and the Komodo dragon are both frightening reptiles. Both have threatning teeth. No one would want to get near these meat eaters. Both can attack humans.

However, there are many differences between these two animals. The American alligator is found in Florida and a few other states along the Gulf of Mexico. On the other hand, the Komodo dragon lives on three Indonesian islands. Alligators grow much larger than the dragons. An adult male can weigh as much as 500 pounds and grows to 15 feet long. But a male Komodo dragon weighs only 150 pounds and is about 10 feet long.

The Komodo dragon is the largest lizard in the world. An alligator is not a lizard, but it is the largest reptile in North America. These animals live in different habitats. The Komodo dragon prefers tropical grasslands. However, an alligator lives near freshwater lakes and rivers.

American alligators and Komodo dragons share a common predator: humans. Alligators sometimes wander far from their habitat and are killed when they get near homes or neighborhoods. Farmers shoot Komodo dragons

Continued on next page

to protect their farm animals from being eaten by the dragons.

   Although these two types of reptiles have many differences and few similarities, I can think of one more thing they have in common. People would not want to have either one living in their house. Everyone agrees they are better off in nature.

## Score 4

This essay is focused and uses strong elaboration to compare and contrast two animals. Similarities and differences are grouped into paragraphs. The voice is lively and informative. Transition words such as *both, but,* and *however* show similarities and differences. Sentences are varied and fluent. Writing shows good control of conventions, except for one misspelling *(threatning).*

## Cats and Dogs

Cats and dogs are alike in several ways. One way is they are both mammals. They also both have tails and run on four legs. A third way they're alike is they both have fur and claws and are tame. Cats and dogs are both domestic and they are both lots of fun to play with.

Cats and dogs are different in several ways. One way cats and dogs are different is that dogs bark and cats meow. Dogs love to run around and play. They like to play catch with a stick, and some dogs like to do tricks. Cats like to sit on the end of the couch and take a nap, but they don't usually like to do tricks. You can take your dog on a walk. When you want to take your cat on a walk, you can't find him or her.

Those are some ways that dogs and cats are alike and different.

Continued on next page

## Score 3

The writer notes many points of comparison and contrast in this essay. The writer is involved with the topic and the structure is clear. Word choice is appropriate and sometimes precise, and words such as *both* and *but* show similarities and differences. Sentences are generally well structured, though there is some lack of variety of sentence types. There is good control of conventions.

## Frog and Toad

The frog has legs built for jumping while the toad's legs are built for walking or smaller hops. The toad lives in a very dry climate, but the frog's skin must be kept moist or else the frog will die. They are the same in certin matters also for example, they are both predaters, but at the same time they are also prey. Frogs are consumed by humans more often then toads are. They both hatch from eggs but the frog's second stage of it's life cycle it is a tadpole while the toad does not.

Continued on next page

## Score 2

The writer provides a number of comparisons and contrasts in this essay. Words such as *both* and *but* are used to signal similarities and differences. The information the writer provides is interesting, but numerous errors in sentence structure, including two run-on sentences and numerous spelling and punctuation errors, account for the low score.

### Rabit or Snake

A rabit and snake have a lot of similarities and differences. they are alike buy habit is one way. (where they lived) They both live in the woods. They also both a pets to keep. The ones that you get from the pet shop. Don't get the one from the woods the could be poisens or have rabies and get you sick.

A rabit hops around and a snake slim, sgwilege threw the grass and dead leaves. A rabit pushes his or her legs back and jumps. A snake is ready to attack, cesplaisey posiens snakes. A rabit acts com and smoth. Rabits sometimes bites, but not usually. A snake on the other hand will bite if disturb.

Continued on next page

## Score 1

Writer makes an attempt to compare a rabbit and a snake. Some details about the two animals are provided. However, numerous errors in spelling, punctuation, capitalization, and sentence construction are confusing and seriously detract from the essay.

**PROMPT** ▶ Write about a real or imaginary trip you might take.

| Rubric | 4 | 3 | 2 | 1 |
|---|---|---|---|---|
| **Focus/Ideas** | Story clearly focused on one event | Story generally focused on one event | Story lacks focus; event unclear | Story without focus; no event |
| **Organization** | Well organized with clear beginning, middle, end | Somewhat organized with beginning, middle, end | Unclear beginning, middle, end | Lacks organization |
| **Voice** | Voice of character or narrator believable and engaging | Voice of character or narrator somewhat believable | Character or narrator lacking distinct voice | Voice of character or narrator not believable |
| **Word Choice** | Uses transitions to show sequence; includes vivid details | Uses some transitions to show sequence; some vivid details | Sequence of events unclear; few vivid details | No attempt to show sequence or include vivid details |
| **Sentences** | Clear sentences, varied in type, including simple, compound, and complex | Mostly clear sentences with some variety | Some sentences unclear, no compound or complex sentences | Incoherent sentences; dull, choppy style |
| **Conventions** | Few, if any, errors | Several minor errors | Many errors | Serious errors that detract from story |

## Field Trip to My Imagination

Have you ever taken a field trip? Our last field trip was to a museum. Robert, Seth, and I headed straight for the medieval display. We were almost as tall as the suits of armor! There were also swords, shields, and goblets. We stood with our noses pressed up against the glass, staring at the chain-link suit.

I stared into the mask. I could imagine that cold metal pressing on my shoulders, the weight of the sword in my hand. Suddenly, I felt the strangest sensation. I was pulled forward by some unknown force.

One second later, I was looking at the knight's mask— from the inside! I could see Robert and Seth on the other side of the glass case. Robert stood with his mouth hanging open, and Seth had both hands pressed up against his temples.

"I'm not looking for a fight," the knight on my left said.

"Whaaaa?" I jumped, turning to face him.

"You got a good imagination, kid. You transported yourself into the armor, but you didn't go far enough to actually make it to the battlefield."

"Battlefield?" No! How do I get out of here?"

Continued on next page

"Same way you got in," the knight said.

I stared at the empty space next to my friends. I wanted to be standing next to them. Suddenly, I felt myself shoved forward.

"Man!" I said, gasping.

"What?" Seth asked, unsuspecting, like nothing had happened. Had it?

## Score 4

This story is well focused and has a clear beginning, middle, and end. The writer engages readers with a question at the beginning and establishes a clear point of view throughout. Specific words provide clear images, and quotations enliven the narrative. Sentences are fluent and varied. Writing shows an excellent grasp of conventions.

## The Camp Ghost

"Gotcha!" my brother shouted, shoving my back as he yelled in my ear. His trick is so old. Every year we take a family camping trip and every year at the end of Mom's story about Harriet, the camp ghost, my brother tries to scare me. It never works.

Well, this year was going to be different. This year I was going to get my brother back.

Harriet was a baker at the camp back in the early 1900s, so while my brother slept that night, I filled his shoes. With flour. As he shook them out the next morning, I creeped up behind him and whispered, "Harriet," in his ear. He said to stop bugging him.

The following night, my brother unzipped his sleeping bag to find more flour sprinkled inside it.

"Harriet," I whispered. He was getting pretty mad by now.

Hours later, I woke up hearing clanging metal. We ran in the direction of the noise. It came from the camp's kitchen.

There we saw a ghostly sight in the moonlight. Pots, pans, and muffin tins all clattered across the counters. Wind blew through the windows, but not enough to set all the

Continued on next page

© Pearson Education 4

supplies rattling on their own. What could it be.

   As if I weren't scared enough, I heard an old lady's voice howl, "Who took my flour?"

   Then I heard laughing from behind the counter. When we turned on the lights I saw the clear string tied to those rattling pots and pans.

   "Gotcha!" my brother shouted.

## Score 3

The story has lively details and dialogue. The voice is involved, and specific words create strong images. Sentences are varied and fluent. Punctuation errors, a fragment *(With Flour.)*, and two incorrect verb forms *(sleeped, creeped)* prevent this story from getting a top score.

## Cancun, Mexico

My family wanted to go someplace where there was gorgeus beaches, coconut trees, beautifull sunsets and a jungel. So my parents decided that our whole family would take a trip to Cancun Mexico.

When we arrived, we were amazed by the beautifull jungel. It had palm trees, coconut trees, and banana trees and was real warm and sunny. My brother and I wanted to explor it, but Mom said, "No, youll get lost." So we didn't go.

The next day we headed out to the beach. The sand sparkeled and sqwished between my toes. My brother and my sister and me asked if we could go snorkeling, and Mom said yes, so we got eqwipment and went out for a while.

Snorkeling is fun but a little difficult. At the beginning. You have to breath threw your mouth not your nose. So you have a mouth piece with a tube that sticks out of the water when you swim around so you can still get air and breath. There is also a face mask that covers your eyes and your nose. It sucktions on your face so water doesn't get in. That's why you have to breth out of your mouth. If

Continued on next page

you accidently breth in it you can fog it up. You also have

flippers. Flippers look a little like frogs feet and they help

you swim faster in the water.

## Score 2

This story lacks consistent focus. There is a clear beginning and middle, but the narrative shifts from a story about a trip to Cancun to information about snorkeling equipment. Voice is interested and pleasant, and there are some vivid details. Sentences are generally varied but include run-ons and a fragment *(At the beginning.)* Numerous spelling and punctuation errors also contribute to the low score.

## Disney World

When it was spring I went to Disney World. I had lots of fun. I stayed in a hotel. Their breakfast was good. Our beds were soft and cossy. I liked to jump from bed to bed. I had my own TV. The front yard was huge. My brother wanted to go so bad. He kept asking when are we going to go. Finally we went! There was thowsands of parks. The funest ride was Expadition everst. Space Mountain was therd best. Rock'n rollen rollercoster was secund best. We did it day after day after day. Then we had to go home. It stunk. At least I had fun.

Continued on next page

© Pearson Education 4

## Score 1

This reads more like a list of events than a story. Everything seems of equal importance, partly because each piece of information is in it's own sentence. Voice is present, but weak, there is almost no variation in sentence structure. In addition, numerous spelling and capitalization errors detract from the writing and contribute to the low score.

**PROMPT** ▶ Write to persuade your teachers to plan a trip to a place you want to visit with your class.

| Rubric | 4 | 3 | 2 | 1 |
|---|---|---|---|---|
| Focus/Ideas | Well-focused essay; clear position | Generally focused essay; clear position | Lacking focus; unclear position | Without focus; no clear position |
| Organization | Well organized with supporting details | Organized; some supporting details | Not very organized; few supporting details | No organization of paragraphs or details |
| Voice | Convincing voice | Somewhat convincing voice | Unconvincing voice | No distinct voice |
| Word Choice | Uses persuasive words and powerful adjectives | Uses some persuasive words and powerful adjectives | Uses few persuasive words or powerful adjectives | Uses no persuasive words or powerful adjectives |
| Sentences | Correct sentences; varied lengths | Most sentences correct; no run-ons | Some sentences incorrect | Incorrect sentence structure |
| Conventions | Few, if any, errors | Several minor errors | Many errors | Numerous serious errors |

## Field Trip to the Capital

There is a city in our nation that every citizen should visit. That city is Washington, D.C. A field trip to our nation's capital would be a valuable educational experience. Our entire class should take a field trip to Washington, D.C.

We may have to travel a bit, but this field trip would still be a good value. Did you know that some museums in Washington, D.C., are free? That's right, free. While we may pay $5 or $10 or more just to get into one museum in our hometown, we could visit several museums on this field trip for $0. We must take advantage of this great deal!

Visiting museums would make this field trip an educational experience. That's another benefit for our class. In Washington, D.C., we can learn about history, art, and space. The Smithsonian alone has exhibits on just about every subject we could ever study. There are also many monuments and war memorials. Seeing these in person is better than looking at pictures of them in a book.

Finally, we could tour buildings such as the Capitol. In these buildings we could observe the people who run our country hard at work. It would be inspirational to learn

Continued on next page

more about our government and how our nation's leaders do their jobs.

How could a principal or teacher refuse this request? Every student should have the opportunity to visit our nation's capital. It would be the most educational and inspirational trip we could take together.

## Score 4

The essay is well focused on one argument. Supporting reasons are organized into paragraphs, with one reason per paragraph. The voice is convincing and informative. Persuasive words, such as *valuable, educational,* and *inspirational,* are used. Sentence structure is varied. Some questions are used to engage the reader. Conventions are correct.

## Texas Library Association

I think the best place for us to go on a field trip sometime would be The Texas Library Association. Here are the reasons why.

The first reason is that the class would get to meet dozens of authors, illistraturs, and storytellers galore! They'd learn a lot about how books are made. The authors, illistraturs, and storytellers also tell about how they got their ideas. It would support kids' ideas of what they'd like to write. They're really nice too.

About half way down the aisles is the place to have lunch. They could either bring their lunch or bring money to buy from the many different huts, sort of like in the cafeteria at school. I can remember the bar-b-que stand, an ice-cream stand, and of course I didn't forget the HOT DOG stand! There are lots of tables, so we don't have to worry about seats.

The class might want to bring something to carry stuff in, because there's free stuff! There are free books, free bookmarks, free drawings, and free posters! Mostly, you can get different kinds of free books. My classmates will love having those book souvenirs.

Continued on next page

> I have told you the three reasons we should go to the Texas Library Association. First, the authors, illistraturs, and storytellers are there. Second, there's a nice place to eat. Last, but not least, visitors get free stuff. Trust me, if we go there, the class will think it's 38 aisles of fun!

## Score 3

This essay makes a good argument for visiting the Texas Library Association. The writing is well organized, with a paragraph and a topic sentence for each of the three reasons, as well as a concluding paragraph. The writer is engaged and enthusiastic and uses some strong and persuasive words to illustrate her points, though she also uses the vague word *stuff* a number of times. There are also a few unclear pronoun referents throughout the essay. Conventions are good with the exception of a consistently misspelled word (*illistraturs*).

### Waterpark

Our class could go to the waterpark on a fieldtrip. We deserve it. We have been working hard all year long.

Everybody would have fun. They could swim in the water and slide down the waterslides. We would have a great time.

We deserve to go to the waterpark. We all did our homework every week. We all worked hard on completing our assinments in class.

I think thats why you should plan to take us on this field trip to the waterpark.

Continued on next page

# Score 2

This essay fulfills the prompt. The writer stays on topic and provides support. However, supporting reasons are minimal; none is elaborated. Voice is flat, and writer uses very few persuasive or powerful words to make her argument. In addition, there is one contraction punctuation error *(that's)*, words inaccurately written as compound words *(waterpark, fieldtrip, waterslides),* and a misspelling *(assinments).*

I think a good class feld trip would be going to mexico, because kids could learn more about the wars. The teachers could learn some more stuff for the next year. you could probily learn more about the Alamo. The mite have some battles still there. New sience triks top. you could learn different langwages there too. See what Mexican history. discover new foods, but there is one bad thing though it takes awial to get there.

Continued on next page

## Score 1

This essay does focus on a class field trip to Mexico, but parts are indiscernible *(New sience triks top.)* or too vague *(The teachers could learn some more stuff for the next year.)* There is no organizational structure and no distinct voice comes through. In addition, a sentence fragment *(See what Mexican history.),* as well as pervasive conventions errors, seriously detract from the writing.

# RESEARCH REPORT

© Pearson Education 4

**PROMPT** Write about an unusual wild or zoo animal. Use sources such as books, interviews, experts, and the Internet.

| Rubric | 4 | 3 | 2 | 1 |
|---|---|---|---|---|
| Focus/Ideas | Well-focused report with one clear topic | Generally focused report with clear topic | Report lacking focus; unclear topic | Report with no focus or clear topic |
| Organization | Paragraphs with strong topic and detail sentences | Most paragraphs with topic and detail sentences | Few paragraphs with topic and detail sentences | Not in paragraphs; no topic sentences |
| Voice | Informative voice | Somewhat informative voice | No informative voice | No identifiable voice |
| Word Choice | Evidence of paraphrasing | Some evidence of paraphrasing | Paraphrasing attempted | No paraphrasing |
| Sentences | Varied, well-constructed sentences | Well-constructed sentences; some variety | Some unclear sentences; little variety | Fragments and run-ons; no variety |
| Conventions | Few, if any, errors | Few errors | Errors that detract from writing | Serious errors that prevent understanding |

## The Amazing Elephant

Elephants are amazing animals, and they deserve to be protected. Their size sets them apart from other animals. Their trunks are very useful. In addition, elephants are kind and caring animals. However, elephants are in danger today. Some people are destroying them and their environment. Everyone must work to save the elephant.

Elephants are the largest land animals. They can weigh six tons and eat 300 pounds of food each day. The trunks of grown elephants may weigh over 250 pounds and measure five feet long. Males have tusks, which are ivory teeth more than six feet long.

Imagine a tool that can breathe, hug, grab, spray water, and make noises. An elephant's trunk can do all these things. Elephants use their trunks for breathing and smelling. Mothers hug their babies with their trunks. A huge trunk can grab and pick up something as small as a peanut. Do you know how elephants take showers? They suck up water in their trunks and spray it over their bodies. A trunk can even make loud noises. The elephant's trunk is an incredible tool! It is a nose, an arm or hand, a hose, and a horn.

Continued on next page

Elephants show kindness to each other. They care for sick members of the herd. Mother elephants protect their babies in the middle of the herd. Sometimes they plaster wet mud on their babies to shield them from insects.

Sadly, these large, amazing animals are in danger. People have taken their land for buildings and farms. Hunters have killed them for sport and for their ivory tusks. Now humans are trying to protect elephants. New laws have created safe areas called reserves, banned illegal hunting, and limited the sale of ivory. We must all work to save the elephant.

## Score 4

Report is well focused and elaborated with many telling details. Each paragraph has a topic sentence and strong supporting sentences. Ideas flow from one paragraph to the next. It is clear that the writer knows and cares about the topic. Vivid words, especially verbs *(hug, spray, grab, suck, plaster, banned)*, add interest. Sentences are well constructed and varied. There is good control of conventions.

## The Marvelous Okapi

The okapi is a really interesting animal because it looks like sever different animals in one. The first time I saw the okapi at the zoo, I thought it was a zebra. Then I wanted to learn more about it.

The okapi has a look that is unique. They have a reddish-brown back and black stripes on their front and back legs. From a distance, the stripes make them look like zebras. The front of their body looks a lot like a giraffe, accept the giraffe has a longer neck. Okapis also have an unusually long tongue. They can lick their entire ear inside and out. They can lick their own eyelids too.

Most Okapis live in the rain forests in Africa. Their color and stripes help camouflage them. They don't live in herds like some other animals do. They mostly live alone or with their offspring. The okapi is a herbivore.

When European explorers in Africa first discovered the okapi, the explorers thought it was a rain forest zebra.

Continued on next page

Others thought it was a rain forest horse. In Africa, they were known as "The African Unicorns." The okapi is now a threatened animal because of shrinking rain forests and poaching.

    I think the okapi is a really interesting animal and I hope you do too.

## Score 3

This report is clearly focused on one topic. Each of the paragraphs of the report's body begins with a topic sentence followed by supporting details. Voice is informed and interested. There is evidence of paraphrasing *(When European explorers in Africa . . . rain forest zebra.)*. Sentences are generally varied and well constructed, though there are a few missing commas. Misspellings *(sever for several, accept for except)* detract little from the writing.

## Wolverines

Gulo gulo is the scientific name for wolverine. The wolverine is a member of the Mustelidae family. Also in the family is the weasel, skunk, and sea otter. Some physical characteristics of the wolverine are it has a stocky body, thick brown fur running over it's hips and shoulders. The wolverine can be found in a variety of habitats, because wolverines can adapt to a vartiety of areas, they just need it to be cold. They dont have a pickey diet they will eat from insect larvae to deer. The woverine is pretty fast for example, they need to be fast enough to chase down and eat a squirrel. My source is Steve Hinshaw the specimim collectian manager at the University of Michigan.

**Continued on next page**

## Score 2

This report has one focus, but the information is not organized into paragraphs. Supporting information is minimal, though the information included is pertinent and clear. There appears to be some paraphrasing *(The wolverine is . . . Mustelidae family.)*, and the writer includes the name of his source as part of the report text. There is one run-on sentence *(The wolverine is pretty fast . . . eat a squirrel.)*, as well as sentences with awkward or incomplete construction *(The don't have . . . larvae to deer.)*. Conventions errors include lack of punctuation and paragraph indentation as well as misspellings *(vartiety, pickey, woverine, specimim, collectian)*.

### The Chimaera fish (Hydrolagus colliei)

They can live up to 2,600 feet down in the ocean. They can grow up to 50 inches (150 cm.) in adult length. It has a venomous spine at the base of it's dorsal fin. Its skeleton's made completely of cartilage and they have smooth skin with no scales. they have 3 rows of permanent grinding tooth plates and there upper jaw is fused with there skull. The fossil of this strange creature date back to around Early Devonian. Their main food source is bottom-living invertebrates. This fish is really cool!

Continued on next page

## Score 1

This report is difficult to follow because technical information is included in poorly constructed sentences. There is a lack of pronoun referents, and some sentences lack number agreement *(Its skeleton's made completely of cartilage and they have smooth skin…; The fossil of this strange creature date back…)* Some source information seems to have been used directly; paraphrasing is not evident. A possessive *(it's)* is inappropriately used instead of a plural *(its)*, and one sentence begins with a lowercase letter.

# REALISTIC FICTION

| Rubric | 6 | 5 | 4 | 3 | 2 | 1 |
|---|---|---|---|---|---|---|
| Focus/Ideas | Interesting selection and characters; clearly focused | Story clearly focused on one event | Story mostly focused on one event | Story generally focused on one event | Story lacks focus; event unclear | Story without focus; no event |
| Organization | Clearly organized using beginning, middle, and end | Organized using beginning, middle, and end | Organized with apparent beginning, middle, and end | Beginning, middle, and end attempted | Lacks clear, beginning, middle, and end | Lacks organization |
| Voice | Voice of character/narrator believable and shows feeling | Voice of character/narrator believable and engaging | Voice of character/narrator believable | Voice of character/narrator mostly believable | Character or narrator lacking distinct voice | Voice of character or narrator not believable |
| Word Choice | Word choice vivid, strong, precise, and engaging | Word choice vivid, strong, and precise | Word choice sometimes vivid, strong, and precise | Word choice adequate | Word choice weak; few examples of strong and precise choices | Dull and/or inaccurate word choices throughout |
| Sentences | Well-crafted, varied sentences | Clear, varied sentences; excellent flow | Varied sentences; some complex | Mostly clear sentences with good variety | Some sentences unclear; little or no variety | Incoherent sentences; dull, choppy style |
| Conventions | No errors; correct end punctuation for declarative, imperative, and interrogative sentences | Few, if any errors; correct end punctuation for declarative and interrogative sentences | Few errors; generally correct end punctuation for sentences | Several minor errors | Many errors, some serious; Incorrect end punctuation in declarative and/or interrogative sentences | Numerous errors; hard to understand |

| Rubric | 5 | 4 | 3 | 2 | 1 |
|---|---|---|---|---|---|
| Focus/Ideas | Story clearly focused on one event | Story mostly focused on one event | Story generally focused on one event | Story lacks focus; event unclear | Story without focus; no event |
| Organization | Clearly organized using strong beginning, middle, and end | Organized with clear beginning, middle, and end | Organized, with beginning, middle, and end | Lacks clear, beginning, middle, and end | Lacks organization |
| Voice | Voice of character/narrator believable and engaging | Voice of character/narrator believable | Voice of character/narrator mostly believable | Character or narrator lacking distinct voice | Voice of character or narrator not believable |
| Word Choice | Word choice vivid, strong, and precise | Many vivid, strong, and precise words | Word choice adequate | Word choice weak, few examples of strong and precise choices | Dull and/or inaccurate word choices throughout |
| Sentences | Clear, varied sentences; excellent flow | Varied sentences; some complex | Mostly clear sentences with good variety | Some sentences unclear; little or no variety | Incoherent sentences; dull, choppy style |
| Conventions | No errors; correct end punctuation for declarative and interrogative sentences | Few, if any errors; correct end punctuation for declarative and interrogative sentences | Several minor errors | Many errors, some serious; Incorrect end punctuation in declarative and/or interrogative sentences | Numerous errors; hard to understand |

| Rubric | 4 | 3 | 2 | 1 |
|---|---|---|---|
| Focus/Ideas | Story clearly focused on one event | Story generally focused on one event | Story lacks focus; event unclear | Story without focus; no event |
| Organization | Organized with clear beginning, middle, and end | Organized, with beginning, middle, and end | Lacks clear, beginning, middle, and end | Lacks organization |
| Voice | Voice of character/narrator believable and engaging | Voice of character/narrator mostly believable | Character or narrator lacking distinct voice | Voice of character or narrator not believable |
| Word Choice | Word choice vivid, strong, and precise | Word choice adequate | Word choice weak; few examples of strong and precise choices | Dull and/or inaccurate word choices throughout |
| Sentences | Clear, varied sentences; excellent flow | Mostly clear sentences with good variety | Some sentences unclear; little or no variety | Incoherent sentences; dull, choppy style |
| Conventions | Few, if any errors; correct end punctuation for declarative and interrogative sentences | Several minor errors | Many errors, some serious; Incorrect end punctuation in declarative and/or interrogative sentences | Numerous errors; hard to understand |

# EXPOSITORY COMPOSITION

| Rubric | 6 | 5 | 4 | 3 | 2 | 1 |
|---|---|---|---|---|---|---|
| **Focus/Ideas** | Clear, focused composition; stays on topic and presents essential information | Clear, focused composition; stays on topic | Clear, focused composition | Composition stays mostly on topic | Some repeated or off-topic information; leaves reader with several big questions | Composition lacking clarity, focus, and essential information |
| **Organization** | Paragraphs organized around a main idea with strong topic sentences and supporting details | Paragraphs organized with strong topic sentences and supporting details | Good paragraphs with clear topic sentences including main ideas with supporting details | Paragraphs organized around a main idea | Some paragraphs with unclear or missing topic sentences, few supporting details | No paragraphs; no topic sentences, main ideas, or supporting details |
| **Voice** | Involved throughout; engages reader | Engages reader; generally involved | Involved; somewhat engaging | Involved most of the time | Tries to be involved | No involvement |
| **Word Choice** | Exact, descriptive; conveys strong impressions | Mostly descriptive word choice | Generally descriptive | Clear language | Some vague or repetitive words | Incorrect or limited word choice |
| **Sentences** | Varied, well-crafted sentences | Fluent sentences; some variety | Some variety in sentences | Little sentence variety | Many short, choppy sentences | Many fragments and run-ons |
| **Conventions** | Excellent control and accuracy | Good control; few errors | Fair control; some errors | Limited control; few errors | Errors that hamper understanding | Errors that obstruct meaning |

| Rubric | 5 | 4 | 3 | 2 | 1 |
|---|---|---|---|---|---|
| **Focus/Ideas** | Clear, focused composition; stays on topic and presents essential information | Clear, focused composition; stays on topic | Composition stays mostly on topic | Some repeated or off-topic information; leaves reader with several big questions | Composition lacking clarity, focus, and essential information |
| **Organization** | Paragraphs organized around a main idea with strong topic sentences and supporting details | Paragraphs organized with strong topic sentences and supporting details | Good paragraphs with clear topic sentences including main ideas with supporting details | Some paragraphs with unclear or missing topic sentences, few supporting details | No paragraphs; no topic sentences, main ideas, or supporting details |
| **Voice** | Involved throughout; engages reader | Engages reader | Involved most of the time | Tries to be involved | No involvement |
| **Word Choice** | Exact, descriptive; conveys strong impressions | Exact, descriptive word choice | Clear language; conveys strong impressions | Some vague or repetitive words | Incorrect or limited word choice |
| **Sentences** | Varied, well-crafted sentences | Fluent sentences; some variety | Little sentence variety | Many short, choppy sentences | Many fragments and run-ons |
| **Conventions** | Excellent control and accuracy | Good control; few errors | Some minor errors | Errors that hamper understanding | Errors that obstruct meaning |

| Rubric | 4 | 3 | 2 | 1 |
|---|---|---|---|---|
| **Focus/Ideas** | Clear, focused composition; stays on topic and presents essential information | Composition stays mostly on topic | Some repeated or off-topic information; leaves reader with several big questions | Composition lacking clarity, focus, and essential information |
| **Organization** | Paragraphs organized around a main idea with strong topic sentences and supporting details | Good paragraphs with clear topic sentences including main ideas with supporting details | Some paragraphs with unclear or missing topic sentences, few supporting details | No paragraphs; no topic sentences, main ideas, or supporting details |
| **Voice** | Involved throughout; engages reader | Involved most of the time | Tries to be involved | No involvement |
| **Word Choice** | Exact, descriptive; conveys strong impressions | Clear language; conveys strong impressions | Some vague or repetitive words | Incorrect or limited word choice |
| **Sentences** | Varied, well-crafted sentences | Good sentence variety | Many short, choppy sentences | Many fragments and run-ons |
| **Conventions** | Excellent control and accuracy | Good control; few errors | Errors that hamper understanding | Errors that obstruct meaning |

| Rubric | 6 | 5 | 4 | 3 | 2 | 1 |
|---|---|---|---|---|---|---|
| Focus/Ideas | Clear, focused ideas showing connections to original story characters, setting, and events | Shows connections to original story characters, setting, and events | Focused ideas with some connections to original story setting, characters, and events | Ideas show few connections to the original | Parody has some unclear or unrelated ideas, characters, or events | Parody lacking any relationship to original story |
| Organization | Well-organized paragraphs that tell events in chronological order similar to order of original story | Well-organized paragraphs that tell events in chronological order | Paragraphs tell events in chronological order | Good paragraphs with events largely in same order as original story | Some events out of chronological order as original story | No paragraphs or events in chronological order of original story |
| Voice | Language and style match the tone and purpose of the original author's voice | Style matches the tone and purpose of the original author's voice most of the time | Language matches the voice of the original author's voice almost all of the time | Language matches the voice of the original author some of the time | Tried to match the original author's voice | Does not match the original author's style or voice |
| Word Choice | Vivid adjectives and strong verbs convey the humor and exaggeration | Conveys humor and exaggeration | Tries to use adjectives and verbs to convey humor and exaggeration | Clear language; mostly using humorous words and exaggeration | Some words that do not match the style or voice of the parody | Incorrect or limited word choice |
| Sentences | Complete and varied sentences | Complete sentences; some variation | Varied sentences | Little variation in sentences | Too many short, choppy sentences | Many fragments and run-ons |
| Conventions | Correct use of complete subjects and predicates | Mostly correct use of complete subjects and predicates | Few errors in subjects and predicates | Some errors in subjects and predicates | Weak control; some errors in use of subjects and predicates | Serious errors that obscure meaning |

| Rubric | 5 | 4 | 3 | 2 | 1 |
|---|---|---|---|---|---|
| Focus/Ideas | Clear, focused ideas showing connections to original story characters, setting, and events | Shows connections to original story characters, setting, and events | Focused ideas with some connections to original story setting, characters, and events | Parody has some unclear or unrelated ideas, characters, or events | Parody lacking any relationship to original story |
| Organization | Well-organized paragraphs that tell events in chronological order similar to order of original story | Well-organized paragraphs that tell events in chronological order | Good paragraphs with events largely in same order as original story | Some events out of chronological order as original story | No paragraphs or events in chronological order of original story |
| Voice | Language and style match the tone and purpose of the original author's voice | Style matches the tone and purpose of the original author's voice most of the time | Language matches the voice of the original author most of the time | Tried to match the original author's voice | Does not match the original author's style or voice |
| Word Choice | Vivid adjectives and strong verbs convey the humor and exaggeration | Clear language; mostly using humorous words and exaggeration | Conveys humor and exaggeration | Some words that do not match the style or voice of the parody | Incorrect or limited word choice |
| Sentences | Complete and varied sentences | Varied sentences | Smooth sentences, some compound | Too many short, choppy sentences | Many fragments and run-ons |
| Conventions | Correct use of complete subjects and predicates | Correct use of complete subjects and predicates | Some errors in subjects and predicates | Weak control; some errors in use of complete subjects and predicates | Serious errors; subjects and predicates not used correctly |

| Rubric | 4 | 3 | 2 | 1 |
|---|---|---|---|---|
| Focus/Ideas | Clear, focused ideas showing connections to original story characters, setting, and events | Focused ideas with some connections to original story setting, characters, and events | Parody has some unclear or unrelated ideas, characters, or events | Parody lacking any relationship to original story |
| Organization | Well-organized paragraphs that tell events in chronological order similar to order of original story | Good paragraphs with events largely in same order as original story | Some events out of chronological order as original story | No paragraphs or events in chronological order of original story |
| Voice | Language and style match the tone and purpose of the original author's voice | Language matches the voice of the original author most of the time | Tried to match the original author's voice | Does not match the original author's style or voice |
| Word Choice | Vivid adjectives and strong verbs convey the humor and exaggeration | Clear language; mostly using humorous words and exaggeration | Some words that do not match the style or voice of the parody | Incorrect or limited word choice |
| Sentences | Complete and varied sentences | Smooth sentences, some compound | Too many short, choppy sentences | Many fragments and run-ons |
| Conventions | Correct use of complete subjects and predicates | Some errors in subjects and predicates | Weak control; some errors in use of complete subjects and predicates | Serious errors; subjects and predicates not used correctly |

| Rubric | 6 | 5 | 4 | 3 | 2 | 1 |
|---|---|---|---|---|---|---|
| Focus/Ideas | Clear, focused ideas within paragraphs with interesting main ideas | Focused ideas within most paragraphs with interesting main ideas | Focused ideas within some paragraphs with fairly interesting main ideas | Focus within paragraphs in often unclear | Letter not focused around one specific idea | No focus or clarity of ideas |
| Organization | Well-organized paragraphs that contain a main idea and details about the topic | Good paragraphs that contain a main idea and details about the topic | Paragraphs with most details supporting the main idea of each paragraph | Some paragraphs missing main idea or supporting details | Some paragraphs show no organization of main ideas or details | No topics or details in paragraphs |
| Voice | Language and style are friendly and informal and match the purpose and audience | Language is informal; mostly matches the purpose and audience | Language mostly informal; generally matches the purpose and audience | Language sometimes matches the purpose and audience | Language often too formal or flat for a friendly letter | Voice does not match purpose or audience |
| Word Choice | Uses vivid adjectives and strong verbs to present clear, fun images | Uses descriptive adjectives and verbs to present clear images | Clear language; uses some interesting adjectives and verbs | Occasionally uses interesting adjectives and verbs | Vocabulary flat and undescriptive | Incorrect or limited word choice |
| Sentences | Well-constructed and varied lengths and types of sentences | Most sentences vary in length and type | Some variety of sentences | Little variety length or type of sentences | Too many short, choppy sentences | Many fragments and run-ons |
| Conventions | No errors in compound sentences and comma use | Few errors in compound sentences and comma use | Some errors in compound sentences and comma use | Some distracting errors in compound sentences and comma use | Errors that may prevent understanding | Frequent errors that interfere with meaning |

| Rubric | 5 | 4 | 3 | 2 | 1 |
|---|---|---|---|---|---|
| Focus/Ideas | Clear, focused ideas within paragraphs with interesting main ideas | Focused ideas within paragraphs with interesting main ideas | Focused ideas within most paragraphs with fairly interesting main ideas | Letter not focused around one specific idea | No focus or clarity of ideas |
| Organization | Well-organized paragraphs that contain a main idea and details about the topic | Good paragraphs that contain a main idea and details about the topic | Paragraphs with most details supporting the main idea of each paragraph | Some paragraphs show no organization of main ideas or details | No topics or details in paragraphs |
| Voice | Language and style are friendly and informal and match the purpose and audience | Language is informal and mostly matches the purpose and audience | Language mostly informal; generally matches the purpose and audience | Language often too formal for a friendly letter | Voice does not match purpose or audience |
| Word Choice | Uses vivid adjectives and strong verbs to present clear, fun images | Uses descriptive adjectives and verbs to present clear images | Clear language; uses some interesting adjectives and verbs | Some words do not match the style or voice of a friendly letter | Incorrect or limited word choice |
| Sentences | Well-constructed and varied lengths and types of sentences | Most sentences vary in length and type | Some variety of sentences; most well-constructed | Too many short, choppy sentences | Many fragments and run-ons |
| Conventions | No errors in compound sentences and comma use | Few errors in compound sentences and comma use | Some errors in compound sentences and comma use | Many errors in compound sentences, including errors in comma use | No attempt at compound sentences or correct comma use |

| Rubric | 4 | 3 | 2 | 1 |
|---|---|---|---|
| Focus/Ideas | Clear, focused ideas within paragraphs with interesting main ideas | Focused ideas within most paragraphs with fairly interesting main ideas | Letter not focused around one specific idea | No focus or clarity of ideas |
| Organization | Well-organized paragraphs that contain a main idea and details about the topic | Good paragraphs with most details supporting the main idea of each paragraph | Some paragraphs show no organization of main ideas or details | No topics or details in paragraphs |
| Voice | Language and style are friendly and informal and match the purpose and audience | Language mostly informal; generally matches the purpose and audience | Language often too formal for a friendly letter | Voice does not match purpose or audience |
| Word Choice | Uses vivid adjectives and strong verbs to present clear, fun images | Clear language; mostly using interesting adjectives and verbs | Some words do not match the style or voice of a friendly letter | Incorrect or limited word choice |
| Sentences | Well-constructed and varied lengths and types of sentences | Some variety of sentences; most well-constructed | Too many short, choppy sentences | Many fragments and run-ons |
| Conventions | Correct use of compound sentences and commas | Few errors in compound sentences and comma use | Many errors in compound sentences, including errors in comma use | No attempt at compound sentences or correct comma use |

| Rubric | 6 | 5 | 4 | 3 | 2 | 1 |
|---|---|---|---|---|---|---|
| Focus/Ideas | Clear, focused narrative with engaging topic and descriptive details | Clear narrative with details relating to topic | Focused narrative with good topic and some details | Narrative attempts clarity by including relevant details | Narrative has some unclear or off-topic details | Narrative lacking clarity or development |
| Organization | Well-organized paragraphs that tell events in chronological order | Paragraphs organized by chronological order | Good paragraphs with events mainly in chronological order | Few paragraphs with events told occasionally in chronological order | Some events out of chronological order | No paragraphs, no chronological order |
| Voice | Lively, engaging voice that speaks to readers | Engaging voice appeals to reader | Lively and engaging most of the time | Somewhat engaging | Tries to be lively and engaging | Neither lively nor engaging |
| Word Choice | Exact, descriptive, and time-order transition words to convey vivid impressions | Uses clear and exact time-order transition words | Clear language; conveys strong impressions and generally suggests time-order | Fairly clear language; suggests time order | Some vague or repetitive words | Incorrect or limited word choice |
| Sentences | Varied sentences, including complex sentences | Good sentence variety | Smooth sentences, some compound | Some sentence variety | Too many short, choppy sentences | Many fragments and run-ons |
| Conventions | Excellent control and accuracy; independent and dependent clauses used correctly | Independent and dependent clauses largely used correctly | Good control, few errors; independent and dependent clauses mostly used correctly | Fairly good control; few errors with independent and dependent clauses | Weak control; independent and dependent clauses used somewhat correctly | Serious errors that obscure meaning; independent and dependent clauses not used correctly |

| Rubric | 5 | 4 | 3 | 2 | 1 |
|---|---|---|---|---|---|
| Focus/Ideas | Clear, focused narrative with engaging topic and descriptive details | Focused narrative with good topic and some details | Narrative is fairly clear with some details | Narrative has some unclear or off-topic details | Narrative lacking clarity or development |
| Organization | Well-organized paragraphs that tell events in chronological order | Good paragraphs with events largely in chronological order | Few paragraphs with events told mainly in chronological order | Some events out of chronological order | No paragraphs, no chronological order |
| Voice | Lively, engaging voice that speaks to readers | Lively and engaging most of the time | Somewhat engaging | Tries to be lively and engaging | Neither lively nor engaging |
| Word Choice | Exact, descriptive, and time-order transition words to convey vivid impressions | Clear language; conveys strong impressions time-order | Fairly clear language; suggests time order | Some vague or repetitive words | Incorrect or limited word choice |
| Sentences | Varied sentences, including complex sentences | Smooth sentences, some complex | Some sentence variety | Too many short, choppy sentences | Many fragments and run-ons |
| Conventions | Excellent control and accuracy; independent and dependent clauses used correctly | Good control, few errors; independent and dependent clauses mostly used correctly | Fairly good control; few errors with independent and dependent clauses | Weak control; independent and dependent clauses used somewhat correctly | Serious errors that obscure meaning; independent and dependent clauses not used correctly |

| Rubric | 4 | 3 | 2 | 1 |
|---|---|---|---|---|
| Focus/Ideas | Clear, focused narrative with engaging topic and descriptive details | Focused narrative with good topic and some details | Narrative has some unclear or off-topic details | Narrative lacking clarity or development |
| Organization | Well-organized paragraphs that tell events in chronological order | Good paragraphs with events largely in chronological order | Some events out of chronological order | No paragraphs, no chronological order |
| Voice | Lively, engaging voice that speaks to readers | Lively and engaging most of the time | Tries to be lively and engaging | Neither lively nor engaging |
| Word Choice | Exact, descriptive, and time-order transition words to convey vivid impressions | Clear language; conveys strong impressions and generally suggests time-order | Some vague or repetitive words | Incorrect or limited word choice |
| Sentences | Varied sentences, including complex sentences | Smooth sentences, some complex | Too many short, choppy sentences | Many fragments and run-ons |
| Conventions | Excellent control and accuracy; independent and dependent clauses used correctly | Good control, few errors; independent and dependent clauses mostly used correctly | Weak control; independent and dependent clauses used somewhat correctly | Serious errors that obscure meaning; independent and dependent clauses not used correctly |

# NEWS ARTICLE

| Rubric | 6 | 5 | 4 | 3 | 2 | 1 |
|---|---|---|---|---|---|---|
| **Focus/Ideas** | Clear focus on informing the reader about a school event | Ideas mainly focus on informing reader about school event | Many ideas in article have focus on informing the reader about a school event | Ideas generally focused around school event | Some ideas in article unclear or off-topic; little information about the school event | Article is unclear and gives inadequate information about the event to the reader |
| **Organization** | Organized logically, no gaps; strong introductory paragraph | Logical organization; fairly strong introductory paragraph | Organized logically, few gaps; clear introductory paragraph | Organizational pattern clear but weak; introductory paragraph attempted | Organizational pattern attempted but not clear; weak introductory paragraph | No organizational pattern evident; introductory paragraph weak or nonexistent |
| **Voice** | Consistently factual and objective voice | Voice presents facts in an objective manner | Usually factual and objective voice | Consistent, but weak voice | Inconsistent voice | No clear voice |
| **Word Choice** | Vivid, precise word choice | Accurate and consistent word choice | Appropriate word choice | Little attempt at strong word choice | Limited or repetitive word choice | Incorrect or very limited word choice |
| **Sentences** | Varied sentences in logical progression | Good sentence variety; mainly logical order | Not as much variety; order mostly logical | Little sentence variety | Too many similar sentences | Many fragments and run-ons |
| **Conventions** | Excellent control and accuracy; regular plural nouns written correctly | Good control; regular plural nouns generally written correctly | Fair control, few errors; regular plural nouns occasionally written correctly | Limited control; regular plural nouns written incorrectly at times | Weak control; regular plural nouns generally written incorrectly | Serious errors that obscure meaning |

| Rubric | 5 | 4 | 3 | 2 | 1 |
|---|---|---|---|---|---|
| **Focus/Ideas** | Clear focus on informing the reader about a school event | Ideas mainly focus on informing reader about school event | Some ideas in article have focus on informing the reader about a school event | Some ideas in article unclear or off-topic; little information about the school event | Article is unclear and gives inadequate information about the event to the reader |
| **Organization** | Organized logically, no gaps; strong introductory paragraph | Logical organization; fairly strong introductory paragraph | Organized logically, few gaps; introductory paragraph attempted | Organizational pattern attempted but not clear; weak introductory paragraph | No organizational pattern evident; introductory paragraph weak or nonexistent |
| **Voice** | Factual and objective voice | Voice usually factual and objective | Generally factual and objective voice | Inconsistent voice | No clear voice |
| **Word Choice** | Vivid, precise word choice | Accurate and consistent word choice | Fairly accurate word choice | Limited or repetitive word choice | Incorrect or very limited word choice |
| **Sentences** | Varied sentences in logical progression | Good sentence variety; mainly logical order | Not as much variety; order at times logical | Too many similar sentences | Many fragments and run-ons |
| **Conventions** | Excellent control and accuracy; regular plural nouns written correctly | Good control; regular plural nouns generally written correctly | Fair control, few errors; regular plural nouns at times written correctly | Weak control; regular plural nouns generally written incorrectly | Serious errors that obscure meaning |

| Rubric | 4 | 3 | 2 | 1 |
|---|---|---|---|---|
| **Focus/Ideas** | Clear focus on informing the reader about a school event | Most ideas in article have clear focus on informing the reader about a school event | Some ideas in article unclear or off-topic; little information about the school event | Article is unclear and gives inadequate information about the event to the reader |
| **Organization** | Organized logically, no gaps; strong introductory paragraph | Organized logically, few gaps; fairly strong introductory paragraph | Organizational pattern attempted but not clear; weak introductory paragraph | No organizational pattern evident; introductory paragraph weak or nonexistent |
| **Voice** | Factual and objective voice | Usually factual and objective voice | Inconsistent voice | No clear voice |
| **Word Choice** | Vivid, precise word choice | Accurate word choice | Limited or repetitive word choice | Incorrect or very limited word choice |
| **Sentences** | Varied sentences in logical progression | Not as much variety; order mostly logical | Too many similar sentences | Many fragments and run-ons |
| **Conventions** | Excellent control and accuracy; regular plural nouns written correctly | Good control, few errors; regular plural nouns generally written correctly | Weak control; regular plural nouns generally written incorrectly | Serious errors that obscure meaning |

| Rubric | 6 | 5 | 4 | 3 | 2 | 1 |
|---|---|---|---|---|---|---|
| Focus/Ideas | Clear, focused composition with many supporting details | Most ideas in composition clear and supported with details | Some ideas in composition clear and occasionally supported | Ideas in composition at times clear | Many ideas in composition unclear or off-topic | Essay with no clarity or development |
| Organization | Organized logically, no gaps; strong, well-supported topic sentence | Logical organization, few gaps; strong topic sentence | Organized logically, some gaps; fairly strong topic sentence | Logical organization attempted; clear topic sentence | Organizational pattern attempted but not clear; weak topic sentence | No organizational pattern evident; topic sentence weak or nonexistent |
| Voice | Engaging; shows writer's feelings about subject | Involved voice connects with reader | Evident voice connecting with reader | Voice attempts to connect with reader | Weak voice | Flat writing with no identifiable voice |
| Word Choice | Vivid, precise word choice | Precise word choice | Accurate word choice | Vague language | Limited or repetitive word choice | Incorrect or very limited word choice |
| Sentences | Varied sentences in logical progression | Good sentence variety in logical order | Not as much variety; order mostly logical | Little variety; attempts logical order | Too many similar sentences | Many fragments and run-ons |
| Conventions | Excellent control and accuracy; singular possessive nouns used correctly | Good control, few errors; singular possessive nouns generally used correctly | Mainly good control, some errors; singular possessive nouns used correctly at times | Fair control; singular possessive nouns generally used incorrectly | Weak control; singular possessive nouns used incorrectly | Serious errors that obscure meaning |

| Rubric | 5 | 4 | 3 | 2 | 1 |
|---|---|---|---|---|---|
| Focus/Ideas | Clear, focused composition with many supporting details | Most ideas in composition clear and supported | Ideas in composition mainly clear, but few supported | Some ideas in composition unclear or off-topic | Essay with no clarity or development |
| Organization | Organized logically, no gaps; strong topic sentence | Organized logically, few gaps; fairly strong topic sentence | Logical organization attempted; clear topic sentence | Organizational pattern attempted but not clear; weak topic sentence | No organizational pattern evident; topic sentence weak or nonexistent |
| Voice | Engaging; shows writer's feelings about subject | Evident voice connecting with reader | Voice attempts to connect with reader | Weak voice | Flat writing with no identifiable voice |
| Word Choice | Vivid, precise word choice | Accurate word choice | Vague language | Limited or repetitive word choice | Incorrect or very limited word choice |
| Sentences | Varied sentences in logical progression | Not as much variety; order mostly logical | Little variety; attempts logical order | Too many similar sentences | Many fragments and run-ons |
| Conventions | Excellent control and accuracy; singular possessive nouns used correctly | Good control, few errors; singular possessive nouns generally used correctly | Fair control; singular possessive nouns generally used incorrectly | Weak control; singular possessive nouns used incorrectly | Serious errors that obscure meaning |

| Rubric | 4 | 3 | 2 | 1 |
|---|---|---|---|---|
| Focus/Ideas | Clear, focused composition with many supporting details | Most ideas in composition clear and supported | Some ideas in composition unclear or off-topic | Essay with no clarity or development |
| Organization | Organized logically, no gaps; strong topic sentence | Organized logically, few gaps; fairly strong topic sentence | Organizational pattern attempted but not clear; weak topic sentence | No organizational pattern evident; topic sentence weak or nonexistent |
| Voice | Engaging; shows writer's feelings about subject | Evident voice connecting with reader | Weak voice | Flat writing with no identifiable voice |
| Word Choice | Vivid, precise word choice | Accurate word choice | Limited or repetitive word choice | Incorrect or very limited word choice |
| Sentences | Varied sentence in logical progression | Not as much variety; order mostly logical | Too many similar sentences | Many fragments and run-ons |
| Conventions | Excellent control and accuracy; singular possessive nouns used correctly | Good control, few errors; singular possessive nouns generally used correctly | Weak control; singular possessive nouns used incorrectly | Serious errors that obscure meaning |

| Rubric | 6 | 5 | 4 | 3 | 2 | 1 |
|---|---|---|---|---|---|---|
| **Focus/Ideas** | Opinion is focused and clearly stated; details all support the opinion | Opinion is focused; details mostly support the opinion | Opinion is well stated; details support the opinion most of the time | Opinion is clear; some details relate to and support the opinion | Opinion is not completely clear; many details are not related to the opinion | No clear opinion; few related or no related details |
| **Organization** | Ideas are presented in logical order, using transitions | Ideas are presently logically, using many transitions | Ideas are presented in mostly logical order, occasionally using transitions | Order is logical; uses few transitions | Order of ideas is unclear; transitions are weak or missing | No logical order or transitions |
| **Voice** | Voice is lively and interesting | Voice is engaging and lively | Voice is generally engaging | Voice is occasionally engaging | Voice is sometimes dull | Voice is flat and dull |
| **Word Choice** | Uses strong, descriptive words | Uses some strong, descriptive words | Uses few strong, descriptive words | Few descriptive words | Flat word choice | Poor word choice |
| **Sentences** | No fragments, run-on sentences, or comma splices | One or two fragments, run-on sentences, or comma splices | Few fragments, run-on sentences, or comma splices | Some fragments, run-on sentences, or comma splices | Several fragments, run-on sentences, or comma splices | Many fragments, run-on sentences, or comma splices |
| **Conventions** | No errors; correct use of plural possessive nouns | Few errors; plural possessive nouns used correctly | Few errors; plural possessive nouns generally used correctly | Some errors; plural possessive nouns used correctly at times | Many errors | Many serious errors |

| Rubric | 5 | 4 | 3 | 2 | 1 |
|---|---|---|---|---|---|
| **Focus/Ideas** | Opinion is focused and clearly stated; details all support the opinion | Opinion is well stated; details mostly support the opinion | Opinion is clear; some details relate to and support the opinion | Opinion is not completely clear; many details are not related to the opinion | No clear opinion; few related or no related details |
| **Organization** | Ideas are presented in logical order, using transitions | Ideas are presented in mostly logical order, using transitions | Order is logical; uses few transitions | Order of ideas is unclear; transitions are weak or missing | No logical order or transitions |
| **Voice** | Voice is lively and interesting | Voice is engaging | Voice is occasionally engaging | Voice is sometimes dull | Voice is flat and dull |
| **Word Choice** | Use strong, descriptive words | Uses some strong descriptive words | Few descriptive words | Flat word choice | Poor word choice |
| **Sentences** | No fragments, run-on sentences, or comma splices | One or two fragments, run-on sentences, or comma splices | Few fragments, run-on sentences, or comma splices | Several fragments, run-on sentences, or comma splices | Many fragments, run-on sentences, or comma splices |
| **Conventions** | Few or no errors; correct use of plural possessive nouns | Few or no errors; correct use of plural possessive nouns | Few errors with the use of plural possessive nouns | Many minor errors | Many serious errors |

| Rubric | 4 | 3 | 2 | 1 |
|---|---|---|---|---|
| **Focus/Ideas** | Opinion is focused and clearly stated; details all support the opinion | Opinion is well stated; details mostly support the opinion | Opinion is not completely clear; many details are not related to the opinion | No clear opinion; few related or no related details |
| **Organization** | Ideas are presented in logical order, using transitions | Ideas are presented in mostly logical order, using several transitions | Order of ideas is unclear; transitions are weak or missing | No logical order or transitions |
| **Voice** | Voice is lively and interesting | Voice is generally engaging | Voice is sometimes dull | Voice is flat and dull |
| **Word Choice** | Use strong, descriptive words | Uses some strong descriptive words | Few strong descriptive words | Poor word choice |
| **Sentences** | No fragments, run-on sentences, or comma splices | One or two fragments, run-ons sentences, or comma splices | Several fragments, run-on sentences, or comma splices | Many fragments, run-on sentences, or comma splices |
| **Conventions** | Few or no errors; correct use of plural possessive nouns | Few or no errors; correct use of plural possessive nouns | Many minor errors | Many serious errors |

**64 Rubrics**

| Rubric | 6 | 5 | 4 | 3 | 2 | 1 |
|---|---|---|---|---|---|---|
| Focus/Ideas | Clear, focused narrative poem with engaging and descriptive details | Clear, focused narrative poem with many details | Focused narrative poem with some details | Narrative poem has few clear details | Narrative poem has some unclear or off-topic details | Narrative lacking clarity or development |
| Organization | Well-organized stanzas, or line groupings, that tell events in sequence | Good stanzas, or line groupings, with events mainly in sequence | Good stanzas, or line groupings, with events occasionally in sequence | Clear stanzas, mostly sequential | Loose stanzas or line groupings, with some events out of sequence | No sequence |
| Voice | Narrative told in an engaging way | Narrative engaging most of the time | Engaging some of the time | Attempts to engage reader | Is intermittently engaging | Reader does not become engaged |
| Word Choice | Exact, descriptive, conveys a vivid impression; good use of action verbs | Clear, precise language, many descriptive words; many action verbs | Clear language, some descriptive words; some action verbs | Includes few descriptive words and action verbs | Some vague or repetitive words | Incorrect or limited word choice |
| Sentences | Excellent control and accuracy; shows break in lines where sentences would normally break | Good control and accuracy; rarely misses breaks in lines where sentences would normally break | Fair control; misses a few breaks in lines where sentences would normally break | Some control; misses many breaks in lines where sentences would normally break | Little control; misses most breaks in lines where sentences would normally break | No control; sentences are broken up and fragmented |
| Conventions | Excellent control, no verb tense errors; narrative poem generally clear | Good control, very few verb tense errors; narrative poem generally clear | Fair control, few verb tense errors; narrative poem clear at times | Limited control, some verb tense errors; narrative poem unclear | Weak control; errors that distort meaning | Serious errors that obscure meaning |

| Rubric | 5 | 4 | 3 | 2 | 1 |
|---|---|---|---|---|---|
| Focus/Ideas | Clear, focused narrative poem with engaging and descriptive details | Focused narrative poem with many details | Narrative poem has some descriptive details | Narrative poem has some unclear or off-topic details | Narrative lacking clarity or development |
| Organization | Well-organized stanzas, or line groupings, that tell events in sequence | Good stanzas, or line groupings, with events largely in sequence | Clear stanzas, mostly sequential | Loose stanzas or line groupings, with some events out of sequence | No sequence |
| Voice | Narrative told in an engaging way | Engaging most of the time | Is intermittently engaging | Attempts to engage reader | Reader does not become engaged |
| Word Choice | Exact, descriptive, conveys a vivid impression; good use of action verbs | Clear language, some descriptive words or phrases; some action verbs | Includes few descriptive words and action verbs | Some vague or repetitive words | Incorrect or limited word choice |
| Sentences | Excellent control and accuracy; shows break in lines where sentences would normally break | Good control; misses a few breaks in lines where sentences would normally break | Some control; misses many breaks in lines where sentences would normally break | Little control; misses most breaks in lines where sentences would normally break | No control; sentences are broken up and fragmented so that it is hard to make meaning |
| Conventions | Excellent control, few verb tense errors; narrative poem generally clear | Good control, few verb tense errors; narrative poem generally clear | Fair control, some verb tense errors; narrative poem unclear | Weak control; errors that distort meaning | Serious errors that obscure meaning |

| Rubric | 4 | 3 | 2 | 1 |
|---|---|---|---|---|
| Focus/Ideas | Clear, focused narrative poem with engaging and descriptive details | Focused narrative poem with some details | Narrative poem has some unclear or off-topic details | Narrative lacking clarity or development |
| Organization | Well-organized stanzas, or line groupings, that tell events in sequence | Good stanzas, or line groupings, with events largely in sequence | Loose stanzas or line groupings, with some events out of sequence | No sequence |
| Voice | Narrative told in an engaging way | Engaging most of the time | Is intermittently engaging | Reader does not become engaged |
| Word Choice | Exact, descriptive, conveys a vivid impression; good use of action verbs | Clear language, some descriptive words or phrases; some action verbs | Some vague or repetitive words | Incorrect or limited word choice |
| Sentences | Excellent control and accuracy; shows break in lines where sentences would normally break for comma or period | Some control; misses a few breaks in lines where sentences would normally break for comma or period | Little control; misses many breaks in lines where sentences would normally break for comma or period | No control; sentences are broken up and fragmented so that it is hard to make meaning |
| Conventions | Excellent control, few verb tense errors; narrative poem generally clear | Good control, few verb tense errors; narrative poem generally clear | Weak control; errors that distort meaning | Serious errors that obscure meaning |

| Rubric | 6 | 5 | 4 | 3 | 2 | 1 |
|---|---|---|---|---|---|---|
| Focus/Ideas | Clear, focused invitation with engaging and elaborate details | Focused invitation with engaging details | Focused invitation with many details | Invitation has some clear and on-topic details | Invitation has some unclear or off-topic details | Invitation lacking clarity or development |
| Organization | Well-organized invitation with good use of paragraphs | Invitation clearly organized using paragraphs | Organized using paragraphs | Organized using paragraphs; some organizational errors | Some organizational problems; paragraphs may be off | No paragraphs; little to no organization |
| Voice | Engaging invitation appeals to reader | Invitation written in an engaging way | Engaging most of the time | Engaging some of the time | Is intermittently engaging | Reader does not become engaged |
| Word Choice | Exact, descriptive; conveys a vivid impression | Exact, descriptive language | Mostly clear descriptive language; conveys strong impressions | Voice is at times dull | Some vague or repetitive words | Incorrect or limited word choice |
| Sentences | Excellent control and accuracy; variety of sentences | Good control and accuracy; good variety of sentences | Fair control and accuracy; some variety of sentences | Limited control and accuracy; little variety of sentences | Too many similar sentences | Many fragments and run-ons |
| Conventions | Excellent control, few to no errors; invitation generally clear | Good control, some errors; invitation generally clear | Fair control, some errors; invitation clear at times | Limited control, some errors; invitation unclear | Weak control; errors that distort meaning | Serious errors that obscure meaning |

| Rubric | 5 | 4 | 3 | 2 | 1 |
|---|---|---|---|---|---|
| Focus/Ideas | Clear, focused invitation with engaging details | Focused invitation with many details | Invitation has some clear and on-topic details | Invitation has some unclear or off-topic details | Invitation lacking clarity or development |
| Organization | Well-organized invitation with good use of paragraphs | Organized with good use of paragraphs | Organized using paragraphs | Some organizational problems; paragraphs may be off | No paragraphs; little to no organization |
| Voice | Invitation written in an engaging way | Engaging most of the time | Engaging some of the time | Is intermittently engaging | Reader does not become engaged |
| Word Choice | Exact, descriptive; conveys a vivid impression | Clear language; conveys strong impressions | Voice is at times dull | Some vague or repetitive words | Incorrect or limited word choice |
| Sentences | Excellent control and accuracy; variety of sentences | Good control and accuracy; some variety of sentences | Fair control and accuracy; little variety of sentences | Too many similar sentences | Many fragments and run-ons |
| Conventions | Excellent control, few to no errors; invitation generally clear | Good control, some errors; invitation generally clear | Fair control, some errors; invitation clear at times | Weak control; errors that distort meaning | Serious errors that obscure meaning |

| Rubric | 4 | 3 | 2 | 1 |
|---|---|---|---|---|
| Focus/Ideas | Clear, focused invitation with engaging details | Focused invitation with some details | Invitation has some unclear or off-topic details | Invitation lacking clarity or development |
| Organization | Well-organized invitation with good use of paragraphs | Organized with good use of paragraphs | Some organizational problems; paragraphs may be off | No paragraphs; little to no organization |
| Voice | Invitation written in an engaging way | Engaging most of the time | Is intermittently engaging | Reader does not become engaged |
| Word Choice | Exact, descriptive; conveys a vivid impression | Clear language; conveys strong impressions | Some vague or repetitive words | Incorrect or limited word choice |
| Sentences | Excellent control and accuracy; variety of sentences | Good control and accuracy; some variety of sentences | Too many similar sentences | Many fragments and run-ons |
| Conventions | Excellent control, few to no errors; invitation generally clear | Good control, some errors; invitation generally clear | Weak control; errors that distort meaning | Serious errors that obscure meaning |

| Rubric | 6 | 5 | 4 | 3 | 2 | 1 |
|---|---|---|---|---|---|---|
| **Focus/Ideas** | Clear, focused narrative with engaging topic and descriptive details | Focused narrative with descriptive details | Focused narrative with clear topic and some details | Invitation has some clear and on-topic details | Narrative has some unclear or off-topic details | Narrative lacking clarity or development |
| **Organization** | Well-organized paragraph that tell events in sequence | Good paragraphs with events largely in sequence | Good paragraphs with events occasionally in sequence | Narrative organized into paragraphs | Some events are out of sequence | No paragraphs; no sequence |
| **Voice** | Engaging story appeals to readers | Story told in an engaging way | Engaging most of the time | Narrative attempts to engage reader | Is intermittently engaging | Reader does not become engaged |
| **Word Choice** | Exact, descriptive; conveys a vivid impression | Conveys strong impressions | Clear language | Voice is clear at times | Some vague or repetitive words | Incorrect or limited word choice |
| **Sentences** | Excellent control and accuracy; all verb tenses used correctly | Good control and accuracy; most verb tenses used correctly | Fair control; not as much variety; order mostly logical | Little variety in sentences; attempts logical order | Too many similar sentences | Many fragments and run-ons |
| **Conventions** | Excellent control, few verb tense errors; narrative generally clear | Good control, few verb tense errors; narrative generally clear | Fair control, few verb tense errors; narrative clear at times | Limited control; errors affect meaning | Weak control; errors that distort meaning | Serious errors that obscure meaning |

| Rubric | 5 | 4 | 3 | 2 | 1 |
|---|---|---|---|---|---|
| **Focus/Ideas** | Clear, focused narrative with engaging topic and descriptive details | Focused narrative with clear topic and some details | Invitation has some clear and on-topic details | Narrative has some unclear or off-topic details | Narrative lacking clarity or development |
| **Organization** | Well-organized paragraph that tell events in sequence | Good paragraphs with events largely in sequence | Narrative organized into paragraphs | Some events are out of sequence | No paragraphs; no sequence |
| **Voice** | Story told in an engaging way | Engaging most of the time | Narrative attempts to engage reader | Is intermittently engaging | Reader does not become engaged |
| **Word Choice** | Exact, descriptive; conveys a vivid impression | Clear language, conveys strong impressions | Voice is clear at times | Some vague or repetitive words | Incorrect or limited word choice |
| **Sentences** | Excellent control and accuracy; all verb tenses used correctly | Not as much variety; order mostly logical | Little variety in sentences; attempts logical order | Too many similar sentences | Many fragments and run-ons |
| **Conventions** | Excellent control, few verb tense errors; narrative generally clear | Good control, few verb tense errors; narrative generally clear | Limited control; errors affect meaning | Weak control; errors that distort meaning | Serious errors that obscure meaning |

| Rubric | 4 | 3 | 2 | 1 |
|---|---|---|---|
| **Focus/Ideas** | Clear, focused narrative with engaging topic and descriptive details | Focused narrative with good topic and some details | Narrative has some unclear or off-topic details | Narrative lacking clarity or development |
| **Organization** | Well-organized paragraphs that tell events in sequence | Good paragraphs with events largely in sequence | Some events are out of sequence | No paragraphs; no sequence |
| **Voice** | Story told in an engaging way | Engaging most of the time | Is intermittently engaging | Reader does not become engaged |
| **Word Choice** | Exact, descriptive; conveys a vivid impression | Clear language, conveys strong impressions | Some vague or repetitive words | Incorrect or limited word choice |
| **Sentences** | Excellent control and accuracy; all verb tenses used correctly | Not as much variety; order mostly logical | Too many similar sentences | Many fragments and run-ons |
| **Conventions** | Excellent control, few verb tense errors; narrative generally clear | Good control, few verb tense errors; narrative generally clear | Weak control; errors that distort meaning | Serious errors that obscure meaning |

# FORMAL LETTER

| Rubric | 6 | 5 | 4 | 3 | 2 | 1 |
|---|---|---|---|---|---|---|
| **Focus/Ideas** | Formal letter is clearly focused | Formal letter is focused most of the time | Formal letter is generally focused | Formal letter is focused at times | Formal letter is lacking focus | Formal letter is without focus |
| **Organization** | Formal letter is well organized; includes salutation, body, and closing | Formal letter is organized; includes the following: salutation, body, and closing | Formal letter is generally organized; includes the following: salutation, body, and closing | Formal letter is not well organized but includes the following: salutation, body, or closing | Formal letter is not well organized; missing one or more of the following: salutation, body, or closing | Formal letter lacks organization; missing one or more of the following: salutation, body, or closing |
| **Voice** | Informative, engaging voice | Informative voice throughout | Usually informative voice | Voice not always informative | Voice unsure | No clear voice |
| **Word Choice** | Uses a formal tone throughout | Mostly uses a formal tone | Occasionally uses an informal tone | Attempts formal tone | Uses some formal, but mostly informal tone | Lacks formal tone; mostly informal |
| **Sentences** | Variety of well-constructed sentences | Most sentences are well-constructed | Many well-constructed sentences | Some well-constructed sentences | Few well-constructed sentences | Fragments and run-on sentences |
| **Conventions** | No errors; verb tenses used correctly | Few minor errors; most verb tenses used are correct | Some minor errors; most verb tenses used are correct | Several minor errors; verb tenses used are generally correct | Many errors; many incorrect verb tenses used | Numerous errors; verb tenses used incorrectly |

| Rubric | 5 | 4 | 3 | 2 | 1 |
|---|---|---|---|---|---|
| **Focus/Ideas** | Formal letter is clearly focused | Formal letter is generally focused | Formal letter is focused at times | Formal letter is lacking focus | Formal letter is without focus |
| **Organization** | Formal letter is well organized; includes salutation, body, and closing | Formal letter is organized; includes salutation, body, and closing | Formal letter is generally organized | Formal letter is somewhat organized; may be missing one or more of the following: salutation, body, or closing | Formal letter lacks organization; may be missing one or more of the following: salutation, body, or closing |
| **Voice** | Informative, engaging voice | Usually informative voice | Voice becomes informative | Voice unsure | No clear voice |
| **Word Choice** | Uses a formal tone throughout | Uses mostly a formal tone throughout | Attempts formal tone | Mostly informal tone; rarely formal | Lacks formal tone; mostly informal |
| **Sentences** | Variety of well-constructed sentences | Mostly well-constructed sentences | Some well-constructed sentences | Few well-constructed sentences | Fragments and run-on sentences |
| **Conventions** | No errors; verb tenses used correctly | Few minor errors; most verb tenses used are correct | Several minor errors; verb tenses used are generally correct | Many errors; many incorrect verb tenses used | Numerous errors; verb tenses used incorrectly |

| Rubric | 4 | 3 | 2 | 1 |
|---|---|---|---|---|
| **Focus/Ideas** | Formal letter is clearly focused | Formal letter is generally focused | Formal letter is lacking focus | Formal letter is without focus |
| **Organization** | Formal letter is well organized; includes salutation, body, and closing | Formal letter is organized; includes salutation, body, and closing | Formal letter is organized; may be missing one or more of the following: salutation, body, or closing | Formal letter lacks organization; may be missing one or more of the following: salutation, body, or closing |
| **Voice** | Informative, engaging voice | Usually informative voice | Voice unsure | No clear voice |
| **Word Choice** | Uses a formal tone throughout | Uses mostly a formal tone throughout | Uses some formal, but mostly informal tone | Lacks formal tone; mostly informal |
| **Sentences** | Variety of well-constructed sentences | Mostly well-constructed sentences | Few well-constructed sentences | Fragments and run-on sentences |
| **Conventions** | Few, if any, errors; verb tenses used correctly | Several minor errors; most verb tenses used are correct | Many errors; many incorrect verb tenses used | Numerous errors; verb tenses used incorrectly |

# SUMMARY

| Rubric | 6 | 5 | 4 | 3 | 2 | 1 |
|---|---|---|---|---|---|---|
| **Focus/Ideas** | Strong summary; only uses important and relevant information | Good summary; mostly uses important information | Fair summary; generally uses important information | Summary includes main ideas and supporting main details | Summary has some main ideas and few details | Does not understand summary form |
| **Organization** | Important ideas in correct sequence | Important ideas mainly in correct sequence | Sequence of events is generally correct | Sequence is generally clear | Sequence isn't always clear | Unorganized |
| **Voice** | Shows understanding of the main ideas by using supporting details | Shows understanding of the main idea | Shows understanding of topic | Shows some understanding of the topic | Lacks understanding of the topic | Does not understand topic |
| **Word Choice** | Uses descriptive adjectives, verbs, and time-order words | Uses descriptive adjectives, verbs, and time-order words most of the time | Uses some descriptive adjectives, verbs, and time-order words | Uses some descriptive adjectives, verbs, and time-order words | Few or no descriptive adjectives or time-order words | Poor word choice |
| **Sentences** | Uses simple and compound sentences | Good sentence variety | Some varied sentence structures | Little sentence variation | Sentences are not varied | Fragments or run-on sentences |
| **Conventions** | Excellent control; no errors | Good control; few errors | Fair control; few errors | Limited control; some errors | Weak control; many errors | Many serious errors |

| Rubric | 5 | 4 | 3 | 2 | 1 |
|---|---|---|---|---|---|
| **Focus/Ideas** | Strong summary; only uses important information | Good summary; mostly uses important information | Summary includes clear main idea and supporting details | Summary has some main ideas and details | Does not understand summary form |
| **Organization** | Important ideas in correct sequence | Sequence of events is generally correct | Sequence is generally clear | Sequence isn't always clear | Unorganized |
| **Voice** | Shows understanding of the main ideas | Shows understanding of topic | Shows some understanding of the topic | Lacks understanding of the topic | Does not understand topic |
| **Word Choice** | Frequently uses descriptive adjectives, verbs, and time-order words | Uses many descriptive adjectives, verbs, and time-order words | Uses some descriptive adjectives, verbs, and time-order words | Few or no descriptive adjectives or time-order words | Poor word choice |
| **Sentences** | Uses simple and compound sentences | Some varied sentence structures | Little sentence variation | Sentences are not varied | Fragments or run-on sentences |
| **Conventions** | Excellent control, few or no errors | Good control; few errors | Fair control; some errors | Little control; many errors | Many serious errors |

| Rubric | 4 | 3 | 2 | 1 |
|---|---|---|---|---|
| **Focus/Ideas** | Strong summary; only uses important information | Good summary; mostly uses important information | Summary has some main ideas and supporting details | Does not understand summary form |
| **Organization** | Important ideas in correct sequence | Sequence of events is generally correct | Sequence isn't always clear | Unorganized |
| **Voice** | Shows understanding of the main ideas | Shows understanding of topic | Lacks understanding of the topic | Does not understand topic |
| **Word Choice** | Uses descriptive adjectives, verbs, and time-order words | Uses some descriptive adjectives, verbs, and time-order words | Few or no descriptive adjectives or time-order words | Poor word choice |
| **Sentences** | Uses simple and compound sentences | Some varied sentence structures | Sentences are not varied | Fragments or run-on sentences |
| **Conventions** | Excellent control, few or no errors | Good control; few errors | Little control; many errors | Many serious errors |

**Rubrics 69**

| Rubric | 6 | 5 | 4 | 3 | 2 | 1 |
|---|---|---|---|---|---|---|
| **Focus/Ideas** | Story has strong focus and details; clearly stated problem | Story clearly focused, with clearly stated problem | Story mostly focused, with clearly stated problem | Story generally focused, problem well stated | Story lacks focus; problem unclear | Story without focus; no problem stated |
| **Organization** | Effective clues in beginning and middle; clear, logical solution | Clear, logical clues that lead to the solution | Organized logically; clues lead to the solution | Organized logically, few gaps in logical presentation of clues | Logical presentation of clues attempted, but not clear | No attempt to logically present events and clues |
| **Voice** | Voice of narrator original, lively and engaging | Lively narrator with engaging voice | Voice of narrator engaging | Voice of narrator mostly engaging | Weak voice | Voice of narrator not engaging |
| **Word Choice** | Precise, interesting words that create vivid images | Precise, interesting words create rhythm, style, and images | Uses precise words to create rhythm and style | Good word choice; few lapses in rhythm and style | Word choice weak, rhythm and style generally lacking | Dull and/or inaccurate word choices; no rhythm or style |
| **Sentences** | Good mix of sentence lengths and kinds, with excellent flow | Clear, varied sentences with good flow | Clear, varied sentences; with some flow | Mostly clear sentences with adequate flow | Some sentences unclear; little or no variety | Incoherent sentences; dull, choppy style |
| **Conventions** | Excellent control, accuracy; correct use of singular and plural pronouns; correct use of reflexive pronouns | Few, if any, errors; correct use of singular and plural pronouns; correct use of reflexive pronouns | Few, if any, errors; correct use of singular and plural pronouns; correct use of reflexive pronouns | Several minor errors; mostly correct use of singular and plural pronouns; mostly correct use of reflexive pronouns | Many errors, some serious; incorrect use of singular and plural pronouns; mostly correct use of reflexive pronouns | Numerous errors; hard to understand; no correct use of singular, plural, or reflexive pronouns |

| Rubric | 5 | 4 | 3 | 2 | 1 |
|---|---|---|---|---|---|
| **Focus/Ideas** | Story has strong focus and details, clearly stated problem | Story clearly focused, with clearly stated problem | Story generally focused; problem well stated | Story lacks focus; problem unclear | Story without focus; no problem stated |
| **Organization** | Effective clues in beginning and middle; clear, logical solution | Organized logically; clues lead logically to the solution | Organized logically, few gaps in logical presentation of clues | Logical presentation of clues attempted, but not clear | No attempt to logically present events and clues |
| **Voice** | Voice of narrator original, lively and engaging | Voice of narrator engaging | Voice of narrator mostly engaging | Weak voice | Voice of narrator not engaging |
| **Word Choice** | Precise, interesting words that create vivid images | Uses precise, interesting words to create rhythm and style | Good word choice; few lapses in rhythm and style | Word choice weak, rhythm and style generally lacking | Dull and/or inaccurate word choices; no rhythm or style |
| **Sentences** | Good mix of sentence lengths and kinds, with excellent flow | Clear, varied sentences with good flow | Mostly clear sentences with adequate flow | Some sentences unclear; little or no variety | Incoherent sentences; dull, choppy style |
| **Conventions** | Excellent control, accuracy; correct use of singular and plural pronouns; correct use of reflexive pronouns | Few, if any, errors; correct use of singular and plural pronouns; correct use of reflexive pronouns | Several minor errors; mostly correct use of singular and plural pronouns; mostly correct use of reflexive pronouns | Many errors, some serious; incorrect use of singular and plural pronouns; mostly correct use of reflexive pronouns | Numerous errors; hard to understand; no correct use of singular, plural, or reflexive pronouns |

| Rubric | 4 | 3 | 2 | 1 |
|---|---|---|---|---|
| **Focus/Ideas** | Story clearly focused, with clearly stated problem | Story generally focused, problem well stated | Story lacks focus; problem unclear | Story without focus; no problem stated |
| **Organization** | Organized logically; clues lead logically to the solution | Organized logically, few gaps in logical presentation of clues | Logical presentation of clues attempted, but not clear | No attempt to logically present events and clues |
| **Voice** | Voice of narrator engaging | Voice of narrator mostly engaging | Weak voice | Voice of narrator not engaging |
| **Word Choice** | Uses precise, interesting words to create rhythm and style | Good word choice; few lapses in rhythm and style | Word choice weak, rhythm and style generally lacking | Dull and/or inaccurate word choices; no rhythm or style |
| **Sentences** | Clear, varied sentences with excellent flow | Mostly clear sentences with good flow | Some sentences unclear; little or no variety | Incoherent sentences; dull, choppy style |
| **Conventions** | Few, if any, errors; correct use of singular and plural pronouns; correct use of reflexive pronouns | Several minor errors; mostly correct use of singular and plural pronouns; mostly correct use of reflexive pronouns | Many errors; some serious; incorrect use of singular and plural pronouns; some correct use of reflexive pronouns | Numerous errors; hard to understand; no correct use of singular, plural, or reflexive pronouns |

| Rubric | 6 | 5 | 4 | 3 | 2 | 1 |
|---|---|---|---|---|---|---|
| **Focus/Ideas** | Song strongly focused, with theme clearly stated in the refrain | Song well focused, with theme clearly stated in the refrain | Song focused, with theme stated in the refrain | Song generally focused, with theme stated in the refrain | Song lacks focus; refrain unclear | Song without focus; no theme stated |
| **Organization** | Logically organized in lines and verses; all verses follow a regular pattern | Organized in lines and verses; most verses follow a regular pattern | Organized in lines and verses; many verses follow a regular pattern | Generally organized in lines and verses; verses follow a regular pattern | Organization flawed; patterns of verses not regular | No attempt to order the song in lines and verses |
| **Voice** | Voice of author engaging and lively; clearly expresses author's feelings about the subject | Voice of author engaging and lively; expresses author's feelings about the subject | Voice of author engaging; expresses author's feelings about the subject | Voice of author mostly engaging; expresses author's feelings about the subject | Weak voice; author's feelings unclear | Voice of author not engaging; no attempt to express author's feelings |
| **Word Choice** | Excellent use of precise, vivid nouns and adjectives to convey images | Good use of precise, vivid nouns and adjectives to convey images | Uses vivid nouns and adjectives to convey images | Good word choice; most words are vivid and precise | Word choice weak; few vivid and precise words | Dull or inaccurate word choices |
| **Sentences** | Each line conveys a complete, comprehensible thought | Most lines convey a complete, comprehensible thought | Many lines convey a complete, comprehensible thought | Some lines convey a clear, comprehensible thought | Some lines unclear and hard to follow | Incoherent lines |
| **Conventions** | Excellent control; no errors; correct use of subject and object pronouns | One or two errors; correct use of subject and object pronouns | Few errors; correct use of subject and object pronouns | Several minor errors; mostly correct use of subjects and object pronouns | Many errors, some serious; incorrect use of subject and object pronouns | Numerous errors; hard to understand; no correct use of subject and object pronouns |

| Rubric | 5 | 4 | 3 | 2 | 1 |
|---|---|---|---|---|---|
| **Focus/Ideas** | Song strongly focused, with theme clearly stated in the refrain | Song focused, with theme clearly stated in the refrain | Song generally focused, with theme stated in the refrain | Song lacks focus; refrain unclear | Song without focus; no theme stated |
| **Organization** | Logically organized in lines and verses; all verses follow a regular pattern | Organized in lines and verses; many verses follow a regular pattern | Generally organized in lines and verses; verses follow a regular pattern | Organization flawed; patterns of verses not regular | No attempt to order the song in lines and verses |
| **Voice** | Voice of author engaging and lively; clearly expresses author's feelings about the subject | Voice of author engaging; expresses author's feelings about the subject | Voice of author mostly engaging; expresses author's feelings about the subject | Weak voice; author's feelings unclear | Voice of author not engaging; no attempt to express author's feelings |
| **Word Choice** | Excellent use of precise, vivid nouns and adjectives to convey images | Uses precise, vivid nouns and adjectives to convey images | Good word choice; most words are vivid and precise | Word choice weak; few vivid and precise words | Dull or inaccurate word choices |
| **Sentences** | Each line conveys a complete, comprehensible thought | Most lines convey a complete, comprehensible thought | Most lines convey a clear, comprehensible thought | Some lines unclear and hard to follow | Incoherent lines |
| **Conventions** | Excellent control; few, if any, errors; correct use of subject and object pronouns | Few errors; correct use of subject and object pronouns | Several minor errors; mostly correct use of subjects and object pronouns | Many errors, some serious; incorrect use of subject and object pronouns | Numerous errors; hard to understand; no correct use of subject and object pronouns |

| Rubric | 4 | 3 | 2 | 1 |
|---|---|---|---|---|
| **Focus/Ideas** | Song strongly focused, with theme clearly stated in the refrain | Song generally focused, with theme stated in the refrain | Song lacks focus; refrain unclear | Song without focus; no theme stated |
| **Organization** | Organized in lines and verses; verses follow a regular pattern | Generally organized in lines and verses; verses follow a regular pattern | Organization flawed; patterns of verses not regular | No attempt to order the song in lines and verses |
| **Voice** | Voice of author engaging; clearly expresses author's feelings about the subject | Voice of author mostly engaging; expresses author's feelings about the subject | Weak voice; author's feelings unclear | Voice of author not engaging; no attempt to express author's feelings |
| **Word Choice** | Uses precise, vivid nouns and adjectives to convey images | Good word choice; most words are vivid and precise | Word choice weak; few vivid and precise words | Dull or inaccurate word choices |
| **Sentences** | Each line conveys a complete, comprehensible thought | Most lines convey a clear, comprehensible thought | Some lines unclear and hard to follow | Incoherent lines |
| **Conventions** | Few, if any, errors; correct use of subject and object pronouns | Several minor errors; mostly correct use of subjects and object pronouns | Many errors, some serious; incorrect use of subject and object pronouns | Numerous errors; hard to understand; no correct use of subject and object pronouns |

# INSTRUCTIONS

| Rubric | 6 | 5 | 4 | 3 | 2 | 1 |
|---|---|---|---|---|---|---|
| Focus/Ideas | Instructions strong and clearly focused, with each step clearly defining one task in the list with time ordered words | Instructions clearly focused, with each step clearly defining one task in the list | Instructions focused, with each step clearly defining one task in the list | Instructions generally focused, with each step defining a task on the list | Instructions lack focus, steps not clearly delineated | Instructions have no focus; no attempt to break into steps |
| Organization | Strong, clear steps of the process are logically ordered | Steps in the process are clear and logically ordered | Steps in the process are logically sequenced | Few gaps in logical sequence of steps | Logical sequence of steps attempted, but not clear | No attempt to place steps in logical sequence |
| Voice | Voice is engaging, friendly, and instructive | Voice is original, friendly, and instructive | Voice is friendly and instructive | Voice is generally upbeat | Weak voice | Voice is dull and/or unappealing |
| Word Choice | Uses strong clear, precise words to convey instructions and images | Uses clear, precise words to convey instructions and images | Uses clear, precise words to convey instructions | Good word choice; instructions are occasionally unclear | Word choice weak; several instructions are unclear | Inaccurate word choice makes instructions hard to follow |
| Sentences | Strong, clear, varied sentences; excellent flow | Clear, varied sentences; good flow | Mostly clear sentences with good flow | Varied sentences; adequate flow | Some sentences unclear; little or no variety | Incoherent sentences; dull, choppy style |
| Conventions | Few, if any, errors; correct use of pronouns and antecedents | Few errors; correct use of pronouns and antecedents | Some errors; many correct uses of pronouns and antecedents | Several minor errors; mostly correct use of pronouns and antecedents | Many errors, some serious; incorrect use of pronouns and antecedents | Numerous errors; hard to understand; no correct use of pronouns and antecedents |

| Rubric | 5 | 4 | 3 | 2 | 1 |
|---|---|---|---|---|---|
| Focus/Ideas | Instructions strong and clearly focused, with each step clearly defining one task in the list with time ordered words | Instructions clearly focused, with each step clearly defining one task in the list | Instructions generally focused, with each step defining a task on the list | Instructions lack focus, steps not clearly delineated | Instructions have no focus; no attempt to break into steps |
| Organization | Strong, clear steps of the process are logically ordered | Steps in the process are logically sequenced | Few gaps in logical sequence of steps | Logical sequence of steps attempted, but not clear | No attempt to place steps in logical sequence |
| Voice | Voice is engaging, friendly, and instructive | Voice is friendly and instructive | Voice is generally upbeat | Weak voice | Voice is dull and/or unappealing |
| Word Choice | Uses strong clear, precise words to convey instructions and images | Uses clear, precise words to convey instructions | Good word choice; instructions are occasionally unclear | Word choice weak; several instructions are unclear | Inaccurate word choice makes instructions hard to follow |
| Sentences | Strong, clear, varied sentences; excellent flow | Clear, varied sentences; good flow | Mostly clear sentences with good flow | Some sentences unclear; little or no variety | Incoherent sentences; dull, choppy style |
| Conventions | Few, if any, errors; correct use of pronouns and antecedents | Few errors; correct use of pronouns and antecedents | Several minor errors; mostly correct use of pronouns and antecedents | Many errors, some serious; incorrect use of pronouns and antecedents | Numerous errors; hard to understand; no correct use of pronouns and antecedents |

| Rubric | 4 | 3 | 2 | 1 |
|---|---|---|---|---|
| Focus/Ideas | Instructions clearly focused, with each step clearly defining one task in the list | Instructions generally focused, with steps defining a task on the list | Instructions lack focus, steps not clearly delineated | Instructions have no focus; no attempt to break into steps |
| Organization | Steps in the process are logically sequenced | Few gaps in logical sequence of steps | Logical sequence of steps attempted, but not clear | No attempt to place steps in logical sequence |
| Voice | Voice is friendly and instructive | Voice is generally upbeat | Weak voice | Voice is dull and/or unappealing |
| Word Choice | Uses clear, precise words to convey instructions | Good word choice; instructions are occasionally unclear | Word choice weak; several instructions are unclear | Inaccurate word choice makes instructions hard to follow |
| Sentences | Clear, varied sentences; excellent flow | Mostly clear sentences with good flow | Some sentences unclear; little or no variety | Incoherent sentences; dull, choppy style |
| Conventions | Few, if any, errors; correct use of pronouns and antecedents | Several minor errors; mostly correct use of pronouns and antecedents | Many errors, some serious; incorrect use of pronouns and antecedents | Numerous errors; hard to understand; no correct use of pronouns and antecedents |

**72 Rubrics**

© Pearson Education 4

| Rubric | 6 | 5 | 4 | 3 | 2 | 1 |
|---|---|---|---|---|---|---|
| **Focus/Ideas** | Problem clearly identified; solution clearly defined with focusing details | Problem clearly identified; solution clearly defined with details | Clear, focused problem and solution with coherent supporting details | Problem and solution stated clearly, and focus is not too broad; adequate supporting details | Problem and solution lack clarity and/or focus; supporting details are unrelated or inadequate | No discernible problem or solution |
| **Organization** | Excellent flow of ideas from problem to solution; effective time-order words organized logically | Good flow of ideas from problem to solution; strong topic sentence; organized logically | Organized logically; strong topic sentences for problem and solution | Organized logically with few gaps; fairly strong topic sentences for problem and solution | Organized pattern attempted but not clear; weak topic sentences | No organizational pattern evident; topic sentences weak or nonexistent |
| **Voice** | Writer is engaging, sincere, and interested | Writer mostly engaging, sincere, and interested | Engaging; shows writer's feelings about subject | Evident voice connecting with reader | Weak voice | Flat writing with no identifiable voice |
| **Word Choice** | Words carefully selected for accurate, precise, and vivid account | Words mostly accurate, precise, and specific | Vivid, precise word choice | Accurate word choice | Limited or repetitive word choice | Incorrect or very limited word choice |
| **Sentences** | Fluent style with an effective mix of sentences in logical progression | Fluent style with a variety of sentence patterns in logical progression | Varied sentences in logical progression | Not as much variety; order mostly logical | Too many similar sentences | Many fragments and run-on sentences |
| **Conventions** | No errors; excellent control and accuracy of possessive pronouns | Few, if any, errors; good control and accuracy of possessive pronouns | Few minor errors; correct use of possessive pronouns | Several minor errors; mostly correct use of possessive pronouns | Many errors, some serious; incorrect use of possessive pronouns | Numerous errors; hard to understand; no correct use of possessive pronouns |

| Rubric | 5 | 4 | 3 | 2 | 1 |
|---|---|---|---|---|---|
| **Focus/Ideas** | Problem clearly identified; solution clearly defined with focusing details | Clear, focused problem and solution with coherent supporting details | Problem and solution stated clearly, and focus is not too broad; adequate supporting details | Problem and solution lack clarity and/or focus; supporting details are unrelated or inadequate | No discernible problem or solution |
| **Organization** | Excellent flow of ideas from problem to solution; effective time-order words organized logically | Organized logically; strong topic sentences for problem and solution | Organized logically with few gaps; fairly strong topic sentences for problem and solution | Organized pattern attempted but not clear; weak topic sentences | No organizational pattern evident; topic sentences weak or nonexistent |
| **Voice** | Writer is engaging, sincere, and interested | Engaging; shows writer's feelings about subject | Evident voice connecting with reader | Weak voice | Flat writing with no identifiable voice |
| **Word Choice** | Words carefully selected for accurate, precise, and vivid account | Vivid, precise word choice | Accurate word choice | Limited or repetitive word choice | Incorrect or very limited word choice |
| **Sentences** | Fluent style with an effective mix of sentences in logical progression | Varied sentences in logical progression | Not as much variety; order mostly logical | Too many similar sentences | Many fragments and run-on sentences |
| **Conventions** | Minor, if any, errors; excellent control and accuracy of possessive pronouns | Few minor errors; correct use of possessive pronouns | Several minor errors; mostly correct use of possessive pronouns | Many errors, some serious; incorrect use of possessive pronouns | Numerous errors; hard to understand; no correct use of possessive pronouns |

| Rubric | 4 | 3 | 2 | 1 |
|---|---|---|---|---|
| **Focus/Ideas** | Clear, focused problem and solution with coherent supporting details | Problem and solution stated clearly, and focus is not too broad; adequate supporting details | Problem and solution lack clarity and/or focus; supporting details are unrelated or inadequate | No discernible problem or solution |
| **Organization** | Organized logically; strong topic sentences for problem and solution | Organized logically with few gaps; fairly strong topic sentences for problem and solution | Organized pattern attempted but not clear; weak topic sentences | No organizational pattern evident; topic sentences weak or nonexistent |
| **Voice** | Engaging; shows writer's feelings about subject | Evident voice connecting with reader | Weak voice | Flat writing with no identifiable voice |
| **Word Choice** | Vivid, precise word choice | Accurate word choice | Limited or repetitive word choice | Incorrect or very limited word choice |
| **Sentences** | Varied sentences in logical progression | Not as much variety; order mostly logical | Too many similar sentences | Many fragments and run-on sentences |
| **Conventions** | Few, if any, errors; correct use of possessive pronouns | Several minor errors; mostly correct use of possessive pronouns | Many errors, some serious; incorrect use of possessive pronouns | Numerous errors; hard to understand; no correct use of possessive pronouns |

| Rubric | 6 | 5 | 4 | 3 | 2 | 1 |
|---|---|---|---|---|---|---|
| Focus/Ideas | Quest is clear and strongly stated; plot is tightly focused on resolving the quest | Quest is clearly stated; plot is tightly focused on resolving the quest | Quest is clearly stated; plot is focused on resolving the quest | Quest is well stated; plot is mostly focused on resolving the quest | Quest is not entirely clear; plot wanders away from quest | Plot has no quest or direction |
| Organization | Events are in sequence, with excellent flow and all lead logically to plot's climax | Events are in sequence, with a good flow, and lead logically to plot's climax | Events are in sequence and lead logically to plot's climax | Events are in sequence and generally lead to the climax | Events are poorly sequenced and not logically connected to the climax | No logical sequence |
| Voice | Original voice that is lively and interesting | Mostly original voice that is lively and interesting | Voice is lively and interesting | Voice is generally engaging | Voice is sometimes dull | Voice is flat and dull |
| Word Choice | Uses all strong verbs and a variety of vivid, descriptive words | Uses many strong verbs and a variety of descriptive words | Uses strong verbs and some descriptive words | Uses a few strong verbs and descriptive words | Weak verbs; few or no descriptive words | Poor word choice |
| Sentences | Uses a variety of fluent simple and compound sentences in a logical progression | Uses fluent simple and compound sentences | Uses simple and compound sentences | Some varied sentence structures | Sentences are not varied | Fragments or run-on sentences |
| Conventions | No errors; excellent control and correct use of contractions and negatives | Few minor errors; correct use of contractions and negatives | Some errors; correct use of contractions and negatives | Few errors; few or no errors in use of contractions and negatives | Many errors | Many serious errors |

| Rubric | 5 | 4 | 3 | 2 | 1 |
|---|---|---|---|---|---|
| Focus/Ideas | Quest is clear and strongly stated; plot is tightly focused on resolving the quest | Quest is clearly stated; plot is well focused on resolving the quest | Quest is well stated; plot is mostly focused on resolving the quest | Quest is not entirely clear; plot wanders away from quest | Plot has no quest or direction |
| Organization | Events are in sequence, with excellent flow and all lead logically to plot's climax | Events are in sequence and lead logically to plot's climax | Events are in sequence and generally lead to the climax | Events are poorly sequenced and not logically connected to the climax | No logical sequence |
| Voice | Original voice that is lively and interesting | Voice is lively and interesting | Voice is generally engaging | Voice is sometimes dull | Voice is flat and dull |
| Word Choice | Uses all strong verbs and a variety of vivid, descriptive words | Uses strong verbs and a variety of descriptive words | Uses some strong verbs and descriptive words | Few or no strong verbs; few or no descriptive words | Poor word choice |
| Sentences | Uses a variety of fluent simple and compound sentences in a logical progression | Uses simple and compound sentences | Some varied sentence structures | Sentences are not varied | Fragments or run-on sentences |
| Conventions | Few, if any, errors; excellent control and correct use of contractions and negatives | Few errors; correct use of contractions and negatives | Some minor errors; few or no errors of contractions and negatives | Many errors | Many serious errors |

| Rubric | 4 | 3 | 2 | 1 |
|---|---|---|---|
| Focus/Ideas | Quest is clearly stated; plot is tightly focused on resolving the quest | Quest is well stated; plot is mostly focused on resolving the quest | Quest is not entirely clear; plot wanders away from quest | Plot has no quest or direction |
| Organization | Events are in sequence and lead logically to plot's climax | Events are in sequence and generally lead to the climax | Events are poorly sequenced and not logically connected to the climax | No logical sequence |
| Voice | Voice is lively and interesting | Voice is generally engaging | Voice is sometimes dull | Voice is flat and dull |
| Word Choice | Uses strong verbs and a variety of descriptive words | Uses some strong verbs and descriptive words | Few or no strong verbs; few or no descriptive words | Poor word choice |
| Sentences | Uses simple and compound sentences | Some varied sentence structures | Sentences are not varied | Fragments or run-on sentences |
| Conventions | Few or no errors; correct use of contractions and negatives | Few errors; few or no errors in use of contractions and negatives | Many errors | Many serious errors |

# FANTASY

| Rubric | 6 | 5 | 4 | 3 | 2 | 1 |
|---|---|---|---|---|---|---|
| **Focus/Ideas** | Situation in fantasy is strong and clear; excellent supporting details | Situation in fantasy is clear; good supporting details | Situation in fantasy is clear; good supporting details | Situation in fantasy mostly clear; some details | Situation is fantasy at times unclear | Situation in fantasy not clear; no details |
| **Organization** | Strong beginning, middle, and end; strong organizational pattern | Effective beginning, middle, and end; organized in a logical pattern | Organized in a logical pattern | Organized in a mostly logical pattern | Organizational pattern attempted, but not clear | No organizational pattern evident; hard to follow |
| **Voice** | Lively, original narrator with engaging voice | Original narrator with engaging voice | Lively, original voice | Mostly original voice | Mostly impersonal voice | Flat writing with no personality |
| **Word Choice** | Strong, realistic dialogue; precise language that creates vivid images | Realistic dialogue; interesting language and dialogue to create images | Realistic dialogue; language that creates imagery | Dialogue mostly realistic; some language that creates imagery | Dialogue mostly flat; limited use of language that creates imagery | Dialogue unnatural; no use of language that creates imagery |
| **Sentences** | Strong, complete sentences; complex sentence patterns; appropriate end punctuation | Complete sentences; varied sentence patterns; appropriate end punctuation | Complete sentences; a variety of sentence patterns; appropriate end punctuation | Mostly complete sentences; some sentence variety; mostly appropriate end punctuation | Many incomplete sentences; little sentence variety; some appropriate end punctuation | Mostly incomplete sentences; no sentence variety; mostly incorrect end punctuation |
| **Conventions** | Excellent control; excellent use of adjectives; appropriate use of articles | Good control; good use of adjectives; appropriate use of articles | Solid use of adjectives; appropriate use of articles | Good use of adjectives; mostly appropriate use of articles | Incorrect use of adjectives; several incorrect uses of articles | Serious errors in use of adjectives; articles used inappropriately |

| Rubric | 5 | 4 | 3 | 2 | 1 |
|---|---|---|---|---|---|
| **Focus/Ideas** | Situation in fantasy is strong and clear; excellent supporting details | Situation in fantasy is clear; good supporting details | Situation in fantasy mostly clear; some details | Situation is fantasy at times unclear | Situation in fantasy not clear; no details |
| **Organization** | Strong beginning, middle, and end; strong organizational pattern | Organized in a logical pattern | Organized in a mostly logical pattern | Organizational pattern attempted, but not clear | No organizational pattern evident; hard to follow |
| **Voice** | Lively, original narrator, with engaging voice | Lively, original voice | Mostly original voice | Mostly impersonal voice | Flat writing with no personality |
| **Word Choice** | Strong, realistic dialogue; precise language that creates vivid images | Realistic dialogue; language that creates imagery | Dialogue mostly realistic; some language that creates imagery | Dialogue and vocabulary mostly flat; limited use of language that creates imagery | Dialogue unnatural; no use of language that creates imagery |
| **Sentences** | Strong, complete sentences; complex sentence patterns; appropriate end punctuation | Complete sentences throughout; a variety of sentence patterns; appropriate end punctuation | Mostly complete sentences; some variety in sentence patterns; mostly appropriate end punctuation | Many incomplete sentences; little variety of sentence patterns; some appropriate end punctuation | Mostly incomplete sentences; no variety of sentence patterns; mostly incorrect end punctuation |
| **Conventions** | Excellent control, accuracy; excellent use of adjectives; appropriate use of articles | Good use of adjectives; appropriate use of articles | Good use of adjectives; mostly appropriate use of articles | Sparse and incorrect use of adjectives; several incorrect uses of articles | Serious errors in use of adjectives; articles used inappropriately |

| Rubric | 4 | 3 | 2 | 1 |
|---|---|---|---|---|
| **Focus/Ideas** | Situation in fantasy is clear; good supporting details | Situation in fantasy mostly clear; some details | Situation in fantasy at times unclear | Situation in fantasy not clear; no details |
| **Organization** | Organized in a logical pattern | Organized in a mostly logical pattern | Organizational pattern attempted, but not clear | No organizational pattern evident; hard to follow |
| **Voice** | Lively, original voice | Mostly original voice | Mostly impersonal voice | Flat writing with no personality |
| **Word Choice** | Realistic dialogue; language that creates imagery | Dialogue mostly realistic; some language that creates imagery | Dialogue and vocabulary mostly flat; limited use of language that creates imagery | Dialogue unnatural; words vague and dull, no use of language that creates imagery |
| **Sentences** | Complete sentences throughout; a variety of sentence patterns; appropriate end punctuation | Mostly complete sentences; some variety in sentence patterns; mostly appropriate end punctuation | Many incomplete sentences; little variety of sentences patterns; some appropriate end punctuation | Mostly incomplete sentences; no variety of sentence patterns; mostly incorrect end punctuation |
| **Conventions** | Excellent use of adjectives; appropriate use of articles | Good use of adjectives; mostly appropriate use of articles | Sparse and incorrect use of adjectives; several incorrect uses of articles | Serious errors in use of adjectives; articles used inappropriately |

| Rubric | 6 | 5 | 4 | 3 | 2 | 1 |
|---|---|---|---|---|---|---|
| Focus/Ideas | Strong, vivid picture of character; many great deeds and exaggerated traits described; many realistic details | Vivid picture of character; great deeds and exaggerated traits described; most details are realistic | Vivid picture of character; several great deeds and exaggerated traits described; realistic details included | Fairly vivid picture of character; some great deeds and exaggerated traits described; some realistic details included | Few details about character's great deeds and exaggerated traits; few realistic details included | No great deeds or exaggerated traits described, story is completely unrealistic |
| Organization | Logically sequenced and organized with strong, clear beginning, middle, and end | Logically sequenced and organized with clear beginning, middle, and end | Organized with clear beginning, middle, and end | Organized with beginning, middle, and end | Lacks clear beginning, middle, and end | Lacks organization |
| Voice | Original voice that is lively, friendly, and engaging | Voice is original, lively, and engaging | Lively, engaging | Mostly lively, somewhat engaging | Sometimes dull, uninvolved | Writer entirely uninvolved |
| Word Choice | Uses many specific, vivid words, with many strong, descriptive adverbs | Most words are vivid and specific, with many descriptive adverbs | Uses some specific, vivid words, especially descriptive adverbs | Uses clear language; uses some descriptive adverbs | Uses some vague or repetitive words; no descriptive adverbs | Inaccurate, limited word choice |
| Sentences | All sentences are correct and varied; few or no short choppy sentences | Most sentences are correct and varied; few short choppy sentences | Many correct and varied sentences; some short choppy sentences | Mostly correct sentences; some variety, several short, choppy sentences | Some incorrect sentences; little variety; many short, choppy sentences | Incorrect sentences; no variety; mostly short, choppy sentences |
| Conventions | Few, if any, errors; excellent use of adverbs | Few errors; good use of adverbs | Some minor errors; adequate use of adverbs | Several minor errors; use of adverbs | Many errors; sparse and incorrect use of adverbs | Numerous errors; few adverbs; adverbs used incorrectly |

| Rubric | 5 | 4 | 3 | 2 | 1 |
|---|---|---|---|---|---|
| Focus/Ideas | Strong, vivid picture of character; many great deeds and exaggerated traits described; many realistic details | Vivid picture of character; great deeds and exaggerated traits described; realistic details included | Fairly vivid picture of character; some great deeds and exaggerated traits described; some realistic details included | Few details about character's great deeds and exaggerated traits; few realistic details included | No great deeds or exaggerated traits described, story is completely unrealistic |
| Organization | Logically sequenced and organized with strong, clear beginning, middle, and end | Organized with clear beginning, middle, and end | Organized with beginning, middle, and end | Lacks clear beginning, middle, and end | Lacks organization |
| Voice | Original voice that is lively, friendly, and engaging | Lively, engaging | Mostly lively, somewhat engaging | Sometimes dull, uninvolved | Writer entirely uninvolved |
| Word Choice | Uses many specific, vivid words, with many strong, descriptive adverbs | Uses specific, vivid words, especially descriptive adverbs | Uses clear language; uses some descriptive adverbs | Uses some vague or repetitive words; no descriptive adverbs | Inaccurate, limited word choice |
| Sentences | All sentences are correct and varied; few or no short choppy sentences | Correct and varied sentences; few short choppy sentences | Mostly correct sentences; some variety, several short, choppy sentences | Some sentences incorrect; little variety; many short, choppy sentences | Incorrect sentences; no variety; mostly short, choppy sentences |
| Conventions | Few, if any, errors; excellent use of adverbs | Few minor errors; good use of adverbs | Several minor errors; use of adverbs | Many errors; sparse and incorrect use of adverbs | Numerous errors; few adverbs; adverbs used incorrectly |

| Rubric | 4 | 3 | 2 | 1 |
|---|---|---|---|---|
| Focus/Ideas | Vivid picture of character; many great deeds and exaggerated traits described; realistic details included | Fairly vivid picture of character; some great deeds and exaggerated traits described; some realistic details included | Few details about character's great deeds and exaggerated traits; few realistic details included | No great deeds or exaggerated traits described; story is completely unrealistic |
| Organization | Organized with clear beginning, middle, and end | Organized with beginning, middle, and end | Lacks clear beginning, middle, and end | Lacks organization |
| Voice | Lively, engaging | Mostly lively, somewhat engaging | Sometimes dull, uninvolved | Writer entirely uninvolved |
| Word Choice | Uses specific, vivid words, especially descriptive adverbs | Uses clear language; uses some descriptive adverbs | Uses some vague or repetitive words; no descriptive adverbs | Inaccurate, limited word choice |
| Sentences | Correct and varied sentences; few short choppy sentences | Mostly incorrect sentences; some variety, several short, choppy sentences | Some sentences incorrect; little variety; many short, choppy sentences | Incorrect sentences; no variety; mostly short, choppy sentences |
| Conventions | Few, if any, errors; excellent use of adverbs | Several minor errors; use of adverbs | Many errors; sparse and incorrect use of adverbs | Numerous errors; few adverbs; adverbs used incorrectly |

**76 Rubrics**

© Pearson Education 4

| Rubric | 6 | 5 | 4 | 3 | 2 | 1 |
|---|---|---|---|---|---|---|
| Focus/Ideas | Strong, clear focus on one event; excellent supporting details | Good, clear focus on one event; many supporting details | Clear focus on one event; good supporting details | Mostly clear focus on one event; some details | Sometimes unfocused account; few details | Rambling account of events; no details |
| Organization | Strong organization with a logical, sequenced pattern | Good organization with a logical, sequenced pattern | Organized in a logical pattern | Organized in a mostly logical pattern | Organizational pattern attempted but not clear | No organizational pattern evident; hard to follow |
| Voice | Original, engaging voice that is sincere and personal | Original voice that is sincere and personal | Sincere and personal voice | Mostly sincere and personal voice | Mostly impersonal voice | Writer does not express personal feelings |
| Word Choice | Precise word choice that creates vivid images | Mostly precise word choice that creates images | Precise word choices | Word choices generally good | Generally vague and limited language | Vague, dull, or misused words |
| Sentences | Strong, complete sentences; varied, well-crafted sentence patterns with appropriate end punctuation | Varied, well-crafted sentence patterns with appropriate end punctuation | Varied, well-crafted sentences | Generally smooth sentences with some variety | Choppy or wordy sentences; lack variety | No sentence variety; many incomplete sentences |
| Conventions | Excellent control and accuracy; excellent use of comparative and superlative adjectives and adverbs | Control and accuracy; good use of comparative and superlative adjectives and adverbs | Adequate use of comparative and superlative adjectives and adverbs | Use of comparative and superlative adjectives and adverbs | Sparse and incorrect use of comparative and superlative adjectives and adverbs | Serious errors in use of comparative and superlative adjectives and adverbs |

| Rubric | 5 | 4 | 3 | 2 | 1 |
|---|---|---|---|---|---|
| Focus/Ideas | Strong, clear focus on one event; excellent supporting details | Clear focus on one event; good supporting details | Mostly clear focus on one event; some details | Sometimes unfocused account; few details | Rambling account of events; no details |
| Organization | Strong organization with a logical, sequenced pattern | Organized in a logical pattern | Organized in a mostly logical pattern | Organizational pattern attempted but not clear | No organizational pattern evident; hard to follow |
| Voice | Original, engaging voice that is sincere and personal | Sincere and personal voice | Mostly sincere and personal voice | Mostly impersonal voice | Writer does not express personal feelings |
| Word Choice | Precise word choice that creates vivid images | Vivid, precise word choices | Word choices generally good | Generally vague and limited language | Vague, dull, or misused words |
| Sentences | Strong, complete sentences; varied, well-crafted sentence patterns | Varied, well-crafted sentences | Generally smooth sentences with some variety | Choppy or wordy sentences; lack variety | No sentence variety; many incomplete sentences |
| Conventions | Excellent control and accuracy; excellent use of comparative and superlative adjectives and adverbs | Good use of comparative and superlative adjectives and adverbs | Use of comparative and superlative adjectives and adverbs | Sparse and incorrect use of comparative and superlative adjectives and adverbs | Serious errors in use of comparative and superlative adjectives and adverbs |

| Rubric | 4 | 3 | 2 | 1 |
|---|---|---|---|---|
| Focus/Ideas | Clear focus on one event; good supporting details | Mostly clear focus on one event; some details | Sometimes unfocused account; few details | Rambling account of events; no details |
| Organization | Organized in a logical pattern | Organized in a mostly logical pattern | Organizational pattern attempted but not clear | No organizational pattern evident; hard to follow |
| Voice | Sincere and personal voice | Mostly sincere and personal voice | Mostly impersonal voice | Writer does not express personal feelings |
| Word Choice | Vivid, precise word choices | Word choices generally good | Generally vague and limited language | Vague, dull, or misused words |
| Sentences | Varied, well-crafted sentences | Generally smooth sentences with some variety | Choppy or wordy sentences; lack variety | No sentence variety; many incomplete sentences |
| Conventions | Excellent use of comparative and superlative adjectives and adverbs | Good use of comparative and superlative adjectives and adverbs | Sparse and incorrect use of comparative and superlative adjectives and adverbs | Serious errors in use of comparative and superlative adjectives and adverbs |

| Rubric | 6 | 5 | 4 | 3 | 2 | 1 |
|---|---|---|---|---|---|---|
| Focus/Ideas | Strong, clear focus on one event; well supported | Fairly strong, clear focus on one event; good support | Clear focus on one event | Mostly clear focus on one event | Sometimes unfocused account | Several ideas with no focus |
| Organization | Smooth, logical flow of ideas; organized in a logical time-ordered pattern; excellent supporting details | Smooth flow of ideas; organized in a time-ordered pattern; good supporting details | Organized in a time-ordered pattern; adequate supporting details | Organized in a mostly time-ordered pattern; some supporting details | Organizational pattern attempted, but not clear; few supporting details | No organizational pattern evident; hard to follow; no supporting details |
| Voice | Strong convincing ideas; very informative | Very convincing; good information | Convincing and informative | Mostly convincing; some information provided | Somewhat convincing; few facts included | Unconvincing, no facts included |
| Word Choice | Vivid, precise word choice; excellent use of persuasive language | Precise word choice; good use of persuasive language | Precise word choice; adequate use of persuasive language | Word choice generally good; some use of persuasive language | Generally vague language; little use of persuasive language | Vague, incorrect, or confusing word choice; no use of persuasive language |
| Sentences | Varied, well-crafted sentences; shows strong, clear purpose for writing | Many varied, well-crafted sentences; shows solid, clear purpose for writing | Mostly varied sentences; shows solid, clear purpose for writing | Some variety in sentences; mostly indicate clear purpose for writing | Sentences lack variety; limited indication of purpose for writing | No sentence variety; no indication of purpose for writing |
| Conventions | Excellent use of time-order and transition words and phrases | Good use of time-order and transition words and phrases | Adequate use of time-order and transition words and phrases | Some use of time-order and transition words and phrases | Incorrect use of time-order and transition words and phrases | Serious errors in use of time-order and transition words and phrases |

| Rubric | 5 | 4 | 3 | 2 | 1 |
|---|---|---|---|---|---|
| Focus/Ideas | Strong, clear focus on one event; well supported | Clear focus on one event | Mostly clear focus on one event | Sometimes unfocused account | Several ideas with no focus |
| Organization | Smooth, logical flow of ideas; organized in a logical time-ordered pattern; excellent supporting details | Organized in a time-ordered pattern; good supporting details | Organized in a mostly time-ordered pattern; some supporting details | Organizational pattern attempted, but not clear; few supporting details | No organizational pattern evident; hard to follow; no supporting details |
| Voice | Strong convincing ideas; very informative | Convincing and informative | Mostly convincing; some information provided | Somewhat convincing; few facts included | Unconvincing; no facts included |
| Word Choice | Vivid, precise word choice; excellent use of persuasive language | Precise word choice; good use of persuasive language | Word choice generally good; some use of persuasive language | Generally vague language; little use of persuasive language | Vague, incorrect, or confusing word choice; no use of persuasive language |
| Sentences | Varied, well-crafted sentences; shows strong, clear purpose for writing | Some varied, well-crafted sentences; shows clear purpose for writing | Some variety in sentences; mostly indicate clear purpose for writing | Sentences lack variety; limited indication of purpose for writing | No sentence variety; no indication of purpose for writing |
| Conventions | Excellent use of time-order and transition words and phrases | Good use of time-order and transition words and phrases | Some use of time-order and transition words and phrases | Incorrect use of time-order and transition words and phrases | Serious errors in use of time-order and transition words and phrases |

| Rubric | 4 | 3 | 2 | 1 |
|---|---|---|---|---|
| Focus/Ideas | Clear focus on one event | Mostly clear focus on one event | Sometimes unfocused account | Several ideas with no focus |
| Organization | Organized in a time-ordered pattern; good supporting details | Organized in a mostly time-ordered pattern; some supporting details | Organizational pattern attempted, but not clear; few supporting details | No organizational pattern evident; hard to follow; no supporting details |
| Voice | Convincing and informative | Mostly convincing; some information provided | Somewhat convincing; few facts included | Unconvincing; no facts included |
| Word Choice | Precise word choice; excellent use of persuasive language | Word choice generally good; good use of persuasive language | Generally vague language; some use of persuasive language | Vague, incorrect, or confusing word choice; no use of persuasive language |
| Sentences | Varied, well-crafted sentences; shows clear purpose for writing | Some variety in sentences; mostly indicate clear purpose for writing | Sentences lack variety; limited indication of purpose for writing | No sentence variety; no indication of purpose for writing |
| Conventions | Excellent use of time-order and transition words and phrases | Good use of time-order and transition words and phrases | Incorrect use of time-order and transition words and phrases | Serious errors in use of time-order and transition words and phrases |

| Rubric | 6 | 5 | 4 | 3 | 2 | 1 |
|---|---|---|---|---|---|---|
| Focus/Ideas | Excellent, focused narrative with many telling details | Good, focused narrative with many details | Clear narrative with narrow topic | Mostly limited topic | Unclear account; topic rather broad | Confusing account; topic very broad |
| Organization | Events well sequenced with time-ordered words; strong ending | Clearly sequenced with time-ordered words | Organized in a time-order sequence | Organized in a mostly time-order sequence | Sequence isn't always clear | Unorganized |
| Voice | Natural-sounding, sincere, first person account | Pleasant, but not quite natural-sounding, sincere, first person account | Sincere first person account | Mostly sincere first person account | Writer expresses few feelings | Writer does not express feelings |
| Word Choice | Vivid, specific language that describes feelings | Specific language that describes feelings | Good use of describing words | Use of describing words mostly accurate | Some use of describing words | No use of describing words |
| Sentences | Clear, varied sentences with excellent flow | Clear sentences with good flow | Smooth sentences with some flow | Mostly smooth sentences with some flow | Many short sentences | Mostly short, choppy sentences |
| Conventions | Few, if any errors; excellent use of prepositional phrases | Few minor errors; good use of prepositional phrases | Several minor errors; good use of prepositional phrases | Use of prepositional phrases mostly correct | Little use of prepositional phrases | Incorrect use of prepositional phrases |

| Rubric | 5 | 4 | 3 | 2 | 1 |
|---|---|---|---|---|---|
| Focus/Ideas | Excellent, focused narrative with many telling details | Clear narrative with narrow topic | Mostly limited topic | Unclear account; topic rather broad | Confusing account; topic very broad |
| Organization | Events well sequenced with time-ordered words; strong ending | Organized in a time-order sequence | Organized in a mostly time-order sequence | Sequence isn't always clear | Unorganized |
| Voice | Natural-sounding, sincere, first person account | Sincere first person account | Mostly sincere first person account | Writer expresses few feelings | Writer does not express feelings |
| Word Choice | Vivid, specific language that describes feelings | Good use of describing words | Adequate use of describing words | Some use of describing words | No use of describing words |
| Sentences | Clear, varied sentences with excellent flow | Smooth sentence flow | Mostly smooth sentence flow | Many short sentences | Mostly short, choppy sentences |
| Conventions | Few, if any errors; excellent use of prepositional phrases | Good use of prepositional phrases | Use of prepositional phrases mostly correct | Little use of prepositional phrases | Incorrect use of prepositional phrases |

| Rubric | 4 | 3 | 2 | 1 |
|---|---|---|---|---|
| Focus/Ideas | Clear narrative with narrow topic | Mostly limited topic | Unclear account; topic rather broad | Confusing account; topic very broad |
| Organization | Organized in a time-order sequence | Organized in a mostly time-order sequence | Sequence isn't always clear | Unorganized |
| Voice | Sincere first person account | Mostly sincere first person account | Writer expresses few feelings | Writer does not express feelings |
| Word Choice | Excellent use of describing words | Good use of describing words | Some use of describing words | No use of describing words |
| Sentences | Smooth sentence flow | Mostly smooth sentence flow | Many short sentences | Mostly short, choppy sentences |
| Conventions | Excellent use of prepositional phrases | Good use of prepositional phrases; mostly correct | Little use of prepositional phrases | Incorrect use of prepositional phrases |

# CAUSE-AND-EFFECT ESSAY

| Rubric | 6 | 5 | 4 | 3 | 2 | 1 |
|---|---|---|---|---|---|---|
| **Focus/Ideas** | Cause-and-effect essay is clearly focused | Cause-and-effect essay is mostly clear and focused | Cause-and-effect essay is generally focused | Cause-and-effect essay fairly clear | Cause-and-effect essay lacking focus | Cause-and-effect essay without focus |
| **Organization** | Causes and effects are well organized; ends by skillfully reflecting on the causes and effects | Causes and effects are mostly connected; ends with good reflections on the causes and effects | Causes and effects are organized; ends with some reflections on the causes and effects | Causes and effects are organized; ends with little reflection on the causes and effects | Few causes and effects; little organization; end is vague | No causes or effects stated; no organization; no ending |
| **Voice** | Informative, engaging voice | Writer mostly informative and engaging | Some use of informative and engaging voice | Usually informative voice | Voice unsure | No clear voice |
| **Word Choice** | Skillfully uses words to signal cause and effect; new terms are clearly defined | Most words signal cause and effect; most new terms are defined | Uses words to signal cause and effect; many new terms are defined | Uses words to signal cause and effect; limited definition of new terms | Few signal words; few new terms defined | No signal words; new terms are not defined |
| **Sentences** | Strong, complete sentences; variety of well-constructed sentences | Complete sentences; good variety of sentence patterns | Solid variety of sentences | Limited variety of sentences | Few well-constructed sentences | Fragments and run-on sentences |
| **Conventions** | Few, if any errors; excellent control; excellent use of conjunctions | Few errors; good control; good use of conjunctions | Some errors; most conjunctions are used correctly | Several errors; most conjunctions are used correctly | Many errors; many incorrect uses of conjunctions | Numerous errors; conjunctions are used incorrectly |

| Rubric | 5 | 4 | 3 | 2 | 1 |
|---|---|---|---|---|---|
| **Focus/Ideas** | Cause-and-effect essay is clearly focused | Cause-and-effect essay is mostly focused | Cause-and-effect essay generally focused | Cause-and-effect essay lacking focus | Cause-and-effect essay without focus |
| **Organization** | Causes and effects are well organized; ends by skillfully reflecting on the causes and effects | Causes and effects are organized; ends with reflections on the causes and effects | Causes and effects are organized; ends with little reflection on the causes and effects | Few causes and effects; little organization; end is vague | No causes or effects stated; no organization; no ending |
| **Voice** | Informative, engaging voice | Some use of informative and engaging voice | Usually informative voice | Voice unsure | No clear voice |
| **Word Choice** | Skillfully uses words to signal cause and effect; new terms are clearly defined | Uses words to signal cause and effect; many new terms are defined | Some words to signal cause and effect; limited definition of new terms | Few signal words; few new terms are defined | No signal words; new terms are not defined |
| **Sentences** | Strong, complete sentences; variety of well-constructed sentences | Most sentences have variety and are well-constructed | Limited variety of sentences | Few well-constructed sentences | Fragments and run-on sentences |
| **Conventions** | Few, if any, errors; excellent control; excellent use of conjunctions | Several minor errors; most conjunctions are used correctly | Several errors; some conjunctions are used correctly | Many errors; many incorrect uses of conjunctions | Numerous errors; conjunctions are used incorrectly |

| Rubric | 4 | 3 | 2 | 1 |
|---|---|---|---|---|
| **Focus/Ideas** | Cause-and-effect essay is clearly focused | Cause-and-effect essay generally focused | Cause-and-effect essay lacking focus | Cause-and-effect essay without focus |
| **Organization** | Causes and effects are well organized; ends by skillfully reflecting on causes and effects | Causes and effects are organized; ends by reflecting on causes and effects | Few causes and effects; little organization; end is vague | No causes or effects stated; no organization; no ending |
| **Voice** | Informative, engaging voice | Usually informative voice | Voice unsure | No clear voice |
| **Word Choice** | Uses words to signal cause and effect; new terms are defined | Some words to signal cause and effect; new terms are defined | Few signal words; few new terms are defined | No signal words; new terms are not defined |
| **Sentences** | Variety of well-constructed sentences | Mostly well-constructed sentences | Few well-constructed sentences | Fragments and run-on sentences |
| **Conventions** | Few, if any, errors; conjunctions are used correctly | Several minor errors; most conjunctions are used correctly | Many errors; many incorrect uses of conjunctions | Numerous errors; conjunctions are used incorrectly |

**80 Rubrics**

| Rubric | 6 | 5 | 4 | 3 | 2 | 1 |
|---|---|---|---|---|---|---|
| Focus/Ideas | Book clearly described in review; strong, logical focus | Book described in review; logical focus | Book review clearly focused | Book review generally focused | Book review lacking focus | Book review without focus |
| Organization | Well organized; clearly presents the author's message and opinions | Organized; clearly presents the author's message and opinions | Organized; presents the author's message and an opinion | Book review is generally organized; presents a message and an opinion | Book review has little organization; presents a message and an unsupported opinion | No organization; no message; no opinion |
| Voice | Strongly engaging; clearly shows writer's feelings | Engaging throughout; shows writer's feelings | Engaging; shows writer's feelings about the book | Clear voice that connects with reader | Voice unsure | No identifiable voice |
| Word Choice | Vastly varied descriptive adjectives, adverbs, prepositional and appositive phrases | Many varied descriptive adjectives, adverbs, prepositional and appositive phrases | Uses varied descriptive adjectives, adverbs, prepositional and appositive phrases | Some vivid adjectives and adverbs | Few adjectives; no adverbs | No descriptive words |
| Sentences | Fluent style; well-constructed sentences, with varied beginnings | Fluent style; many well-constructed sentences, with varied beginnings | Mostly correctly-constructed sentences, with varied beginnings | Some well-constructed sentences; some beginnings are varied | Few well-constructed sentences; beginnings are all the same | Fragments and run-on sentences |
| Conventions | Excellent control; capitalizations and abbreviations are all used correctly | Good control; capitalizations and abbreviations are used correctly | Several minor errors; most capitalizations and abbreviations are used correctly | Many minor errors; most capitalizations and abbreviations are correct | Many errors; many incorrect uses of capitalization and abbreviations | Numerous errors in capitalization and abbreviations |

| Rubric | 5 | 4 | 3 | 2 | 1 |
|---|---|---|---|---|---|
| Focus/Ideas | Book clearly described in review; strong, logical focus | Book review clearly focused | Book review generally focused | Book review lacking focus | Book review without focus |
| Organization | Well organized; clearly presents the author's message and opinions | Well organized; presents the author's message and opinion | Book review is somewhat organized; presents a message and an opinion | Book review has little organization; presents a message and an unsupported opinion | No organization; no message; no opinion |
| Voice | Strongly engaging; clearly shows writer's feelings about the book | Engaging; shows writer's feelings about the book | Clear voice that connects with reader | Voice unsure | No identifiable voice |
| Word Choice | Vastly varied descriptive adjectives, adverbs, prepositional and appositive phrases | Many varied descriptive adjectives, adverbs, prepositional and appositive phrases | Some vivid adjectives and adverbs | Few adjectives; no adverbs | No descriptive words |
| Sentences | Fluent style; well-constructed sentences with varied beginnings | Well-constructed sentences with varied beginnings | Mostly well-constructed sentences; some beginnings are varied | Few well-constructed sentences; beginnings are all the same | Fragments and run-on sentences |
| Conventions | Excellent control; capitalizations and abbreviations are all used correctly | Several minor errors; most capitalizations and abbreviations are used correctly | Many minor errors; capitalizations and abbreviations are mostly correct | Many errors; many incorrect uses of capitalization and abbreviations | Numerous errors in capitalization and abbreviations |

| Rubric | 4 | 3 | 2 | 1 |
|---|---|---|---|---|
| Focus/Ideas | Book review clearly focused | Book review generally focused | Book review lacking focus | Book review without focus |
| Organization | Book review is well organized; it presents the author's message and a valid opinion | Book review is organized; presents a message and an opinion | Book review has little organization; presents a message and an unsupported opinion | No organization; no message; no opinion |
| Voice | Engaging; shows writer's feelings about the book | Clear voice that connects with reader | Voice unsure | No identifiable voice |
| Word Choice | Many varied descriptive adjectives, adverbs, prepositional and appositive phrases | Some vivid adjectives and adverbs | Few adjectives; no adverbs | No descriptive words |
| Sentences | Well-constructed sentences with varied beginnings | Most sentences well-constructed; some beginnings are varied | Few well-constructed sentences; beginnings are all the same | Fragments and run-on sentences |
| Conventions | Few, if any, errors; capitalizations and abbreviations are used correctly | Several minor errors; most words are capitalized correctly; abbreviations are mostly correct | Many errors; many incorrect uses of capitalization and abbreviations | Numerous errors in capitalization and abbreviations |

| Rubric | 6 | 5 | 4 | 3 | 2 | 1 |
|---|---|---|---|---|---|---|
| Focus/Ideas | Skit with interesting, comic situation; useful, detailed stage directions | Skit with clear, comic situation; many useful stage directions | Presents a comic situation and useful stage directions | Presents a clear situation; most stage directions are useful | Presents a situation that is vague; not enough stage directions | Presents an unclear situation; stage directions are missing |
| Organization | Natural flowing scene is well-developed; clear setting; action easy to visualize | Natural flowing scene is well-developed; setting is easy to visualize | Has one well-developed scene and one clear setting | Has more than one scene; setting contains few details | Has an unclear scene; setting is not clear | No clear scene; no setting |
| Voice | Speech lively, believable, and strong | Speech lively and believable | Speech mostly lively and believable | Speech generally believable | Speech sometimes artificial | Speech unrealistic |
| Word Choice | Vivid, exact, and descriptive; conveys vivid impressions; includes sensory details | Exact, descriptive; conveys many vivid impressions; includes many sensory details | Exact, descriptive; conveys vivid impressions; includes sensory details | Clear language; some vivid words and sensory details | Some vague or repetitive words; few sensory details | Limited word choice |
| Sentences | Strong, complete varied sentences, including compound sentences | Complete varied sentences, including some compound sentences | Varied sentences, including compound sentences | Some variety of sentences including a compound sentence | Too many short, choppy sentences | Sentences lack variety |
| Conventions | Excellent control and complete accuracy of compound sentences | Few errors; commas are used correctly | Several minor errors; use of commas is mostly correct | Several errors; use of commas is mostly correct | Many errors; many incorrect uses of commas | Numerous errors in use of commas |

| Rubric | 5 | 4 | 3 | 2 | 1 |
|---|---|---|---|---|---|
| Focus/Ideas | Skit with interesting, comic situation; useful, detailed stage directions | Presents a clear, comic situation and useful stage directions | Presents a clear situation; most stage directions are useful | Presents a situation that is vague; not enough stage directions | Presents an unclear situation; stage directions are missing |
| Organization | Natural flowing scene is well-developed; clear setting; action easy to visualize | Has one well-developed scene and one clear setting | Has more than one scene; setting contains few details | Has an unclear scene; setting is not clear | No clear scene; no setting |
| Voice | Speech lively, believable, and strong | Speech lively and believable | Speech mostly believable | Speech sometimes artificial | Speech unrealistic |
| Word Choice | Vivid, exact, and descriptive; conveys vivid impressions; includes sensory details | Exact, descriptive; conveys vivid impressions; includes some sensory details | Clear language; some vivid words and sensory details | Some vague or repetitive words; few sensory details | Limited word choice |
| Sentences | Strong, complete varied sentences, including compound sentences | Varied sentences, including compound sentences | Some variety of sentences including a compound sentences | Too many short, choppy sentences | Sentences lack variety |
| Conventions | Excellent control and complete accuracy of compound sentences | Minor errors; commas are used correctly, including in compound sentences | Several errors; use of commas is mostly correct | Many errors; many incorrect uses of commas | Numerous errors in use of commas |

| Rubric | 4 | 3 | 2 | 1 |
|---|---|---|---|---|
| Focus/Ideas | Presents a clear, comic situation and useful, detailed stage directions | Presents a clear situation; most stage directions are useful | Presents a situation that is vague; not enough stage directions | Presents an unclear situation; stage directions are missing |
| Organization | Has one well-developed scene and one clear setting | Has more than one scene; setting contains few details | Has an unclear scene; setting is not clear | No clear scene; no setting |
| Voice | Speech lively and believable | Speech mostly believable | Speech sometimes artificial | Speech unrealistic |
| Word Choice | Exact, descriptive; conveys vivid impressions; includes sensory details | Clear language; some vivid words and sensory details | Some vague or repetitive words; few sensory details | Limited word choice |
| Sentences | Varied sentences in length and kind, including compound sentences | Some variety of sentences including a compound sentences | Too many short, choppy sentences | Sentences lack variety |
| Conventions | Few, if any, errors; commas are used correctly, including in compound sentences | Several minor errors; use of commas is mostly correct | Many errors; many incorrect uses of commas | Numerous errors in use of commas |

| Rubric | 6 | 5 | 4 | 3 | 2 | 1 |
|---|---|---|---|---|---|---|
| Focus/Ideas | Shows an interesting, legendary character or a group of characters clearly achieving a goal; useful stage directions | Shows a legendary character or a group of characters achieving a goal; useful stage directions | Play shows a legendary character or a group of characters achieving a goal; many useful stage directions | Play shows a legendary character or a group of characters achieving a goal; some stage directions | Play presents a goal that is vague at times; not enough stage directions | Play presents an unclear goal; stage directions are missing |
| Organization | Natural flowing scene with a well-organized, logical plot; clear setting; well-developed theme | Flowing scene; clear setting; logical plot; clear theme | Has a clear setting and logical plot; somewhat clear theme | Has a setting and logical plot; theme is vague | Has an unclear setting and plot is not logical; no theme | No setting, theme, or plot evident |
| Voice | Speech lively, believable, and authentic | Speech clear, lively, and authentic | Speech lively and authentic | Speech mostly believable | Speech sometimes artificial | Speech unrealistic |
| Word Choice | Vivid, exact, and descriptive; use of strong verbs; brings events to life | Descriptive; use of strong verbs; no wordiness | Strong verbs; many events are described; little wordiness | Verbs are mostly strong; some wordiness | Verbs are passive; too many words | Incorrect and confusing verb choice; much wordiness |
| Sentences | Strong, complete varied sentences | Clearly varied sentences | Varied sentences | Some variety in sentences | Too many short, choppy sentences | No sentence variety |
| Conventions | Excellent control and complete accuracy of quotations and quotation marks | Minor errors; quotations and quotation marks are used correctly | Several minor errors; use of quotations and quotation marks mostly correct | Many errors; use of quotations and quotation marks mostly correct | Errors that may hamper understanding; some errors in the use of quotation marks | Frequent errors that obscure meaning; errors in the use of quotation marks |

| Rubric | 5 | 4 | 3 | 2 | 1 |
|---|---|---|---|---|---|
| Focus/Ideas | Play shows an interesting, legendary character or a group of characters clearly achieving a goal; useful, detailed stage directions | Play shows a legendary character or a group of characters achieving a goal; useful stage directions | Play shows a legendary character or a group of characters achieving a goal; most stage directions useful | Play presents a goal that is vague at times; not enough stage directions | Play presents an unclear goal; stage directions are missing |
| Organization | Natural flowing scene with a well-organized, logical plot; clear setting; well-developed theme | Has a clear setting and logically ordered plot; theme is clear | Has a setting and logical plot; theme is vague | Has an unclear setting and plot is not logical; no theme | No setting, theme, or plot evident |
| Voice | Speech lively, believable, and authentic | Speech lively and authentic | Speech mostly believable | Speech sometimes artificial | Speech unrealistic |
| Word Choice | Vivid, exact, and descriptive; strong verbs; brings events to life | Use of strong verbs; brings events to life; little wordiness | Verbs are mostly strong; some wordiness | Verbs are passive; too many words | Incorrect and confusing verb choice; much wordiness |
| Sentences | Strong, complete varied sentences | Varied sentences | Some variety in sentences | Too many short, choppy sentences | No sentence variety |
| Conventions | Excellent control and complete accuracy of quotations and quotation marks | Minor errors; use of quotations and quotation marks mostly correct | Several minor errors; use of quotations and quotation marks mostly correct | Errors that may hamper understanding; some errors in the use of quotation marks | Frequent errors that obscure meaning; errors in the use of quotation marks |

| Rubric | 4 | 3 | 2 | 1 |
|---|---|---|---|---|
| Focus/Ideas | Play shows a legendary character or a group of characters achieving a goal; useful stage directions | Play shows a legendary character or a group of characters achieving a goal; most stage directions useful | Play presents a goal that is vague at times; not enough stage directions | Play presents an unclear goal; stage directions are missing |
| Organization | Has a clear setting and logically ordered plot; theme is clear | Has a setting and logical plot; theme is vague | Has an unclear setting and plot is not logical; no theme | No setting, theme, or plot evident |
| Voice | Speech lively and authentic | Speech mostly believable | Speech sometimes artificial | Speech unrealistic |
| Word Choice | Use of strong verbs; brings events to life; little wordiness | Verbs are mostly strong; some wordiness | Verbs are passive; too many words | Incorrect and confusing verb choice; much wordiness |
| Sentences | Varied sentences in lengths and kinds | Some variety in sentences; few short related sentences | Too many short, choppy sentences | No sentence variety |
| Conventions | Few, if any, errors; use of quotations and quotation marks correct | Several minor errors; use of quotations and quotation marks mostly correct | Errors that may hamper understanding; some errors in the use of quotation marks | Frequent errors that obscure meaning; errors in the use of quotation marks |

**Rubrics 83**

| Rubric | 6 | 5 | 4 | 3 | 2 | 1 |
|---|---|---|---|---|---|---|
| Focus/Ideas | Clear narrative nonfiction account of a true event; includes important details | Mostly clear narrative nonfiction account of a true event; includes important details | Generally clear narrative nonfiction account of a true event; some important details | Narrative nonfiction account is often unclear; few important details | Unfocused narrative nonfiction account; details are unimportant | Confusing and undeveloped narrative nonfiction account; no details |
| Organization | Events clearly described in time-order sequence | Events described in time-order sequence | Organized in a mostly time-order sequence | Generally organized in time-order sequence | Sequence isn't always clear | Lacks any logical order; events confused and jumbled |
| Voice | Writer is clearly involved; informative and entertaining | Writer involved and informative | Writer makes a good effort to be informative | Writer makes some effort to be informative | Writer not very involved with topic | Writer totally uninterested |
| Word Choice | Specific language; bring events to life | Specific and colorful language | Words specific and occasionally colorful | Word choice is sometimes unspecific and vague | Ordinary; sometimes vague word choice | Incorrect or confusing word choice |
| Sentences | Varied sentences; short related sentences are combined | Varied sentences; most short, related sentences are combined | Some variety in sentences; few short, related sentences | Occasional variety in sentences; some short, related sentences | Little variety in sentences; too many short, related sentences | Fragments or run-on sentences |
| Conventions | Accurate, no mistakes; correct use of commas; correctly written titles | Few mistakes; correct use of commas; correctly written titles | Few mistakes; mostly correct use of commas; no errors in titles | Some mistakes; some errors in comma use and in titles | Many mistakes; some errors in the use of commas and in titles | Frequent mistakes that take away from understanding; too many errors |

| Rubric | 5 | 4 | 3 | 2 | 1 |
|---|---|---|---|---|---|
| Focus/Ideas | Clear narrative nonfiction account of a true event; includes important details | Mostly clear narrative nonfiction account of a true event; includes important details | Mostly clear narrative nonfiction account of a true event; some details | Unfocused narrative nonfiction account; details are unimportant | Confusing and undeveloped narrative nonfiction account; no details |
| Organization | Events clearly described in time-order sequence | Events described in time-order sequence | Organized in a mostly time-order sequence | Sequence isn't always clear | Lacks any logical order; events confused and jumbled |
| Voice | Writer is clearly involved; informative and entertaining | Writer involved and informative | Writer makes a good effort to be informative | Writer not very involved with topic | Writer totally uninterested |
| Word Choice | Specific language; brings events to life | Specific and colorful language | Words specific and occasionally colorful | Ordinary; sometimes vague word choice | Incorrect or confusing word choice |
| Sentences | Varied sentences; short related sentences are combined | Varied sentences; most short, related sentences are combined | Some variety in sentences; few short, related sentences | Little variety in sentences; too many short, related sentences | Fragments or run-on sentences |
| Conventions | Accurate, no mistakes; correct use of commas; correctly written titles | Few mistakes; correct use of commas; correctly written titles | Few mistakes; mostly correct use of commas; no errors in titles | A lot of mistakes; some errors in the use of commas and in titles | Frequent mistakes that take away from understanding; too many errors |

| Rubric | 4 | 3 | 2 | 1 |
|---|---|---|---|
| Focus/Ideas | Clear narrative nonfiction account of a true event; includes important details | Mostly clear narrative nonfiction account of a true event; a few important details | Unfocused narrative nonfiction account; details are unimportant | Confusing and undeveloped narrative nonfiction account; no details |
| Organization | Events clearly described in time-order sequence | Organized in a mostly time-order sequence | Sequence isn't always clear | Lacks any logical order; events confused and jumbled |
| Voice | Writer is clearly involved; informative and entertaining | Writer makes a good effort to be informative | Writer not very involved with topic | Writer totally uninterested |
| Word Choice | Specific language; brings events to life | Words specific and occasionally colorful | Ordinary; sometimes vague word choice | Incorrect or confusing word choice |
| Sentences | Varied sentences; short related sentences are combined | Some variety in sentences; few short, related sentences | Little variety in sentences; too many short, related sentences | Fragments or run-on sentences |
| Conventions | Accurate, no mistakes; correct use of commas; correctly written titles | Few mistakes; mostly correct use of commas; no errors in titles | A lot of mistakes; some errors in the use of commas and in titles | Frequent mistakes that take away from understanding; too many errors |